Here, the intersection of the timeless moment
is England and nowhere. Never and always.

— T. S. Eliot, "Little Gidding"

Do not laugh! But once upon a time (my crest has
long since fallen) I had a mind to make a body of
more or less connected legend, ranging from the large
and cosmogonic to the level of romantic fairy-story —
the larger founded on the lesser in contact with the
earth, the lesser drawing splendour from the vast
backclothes — which I could dedicate simply: to England; to my country. It should possess the tone and
quality that I desired, somewhat cool and clear, be
redolent of our "air" (the clime and soil of the North
West, meaning Britain and the hither parts of
Europe; not Italy or the Aegean, still less the East),
and, while possessing (if I could achieve it) the fair
elusive beauty that some call Celtic (though it is
rarely found in genuine ancient Celtic things), it
should be "high," purged of the gross, and fit for the
more adult mind of a land long steeped in poetry.

— J. R. R. Tolkien

J. R. R. TOLKIEN

ENGLAND And ALWAYS

Tolkien's World of the Rings

by
JARED LOBDELL

WILLIAM B. EERDMANS PUBLISHING COMPANY

Library of Congress Cataloging in Publication Data
Lobdell, Jared, 1937-
  England and always.

  Bibliography: p. 93.
  1. Tolkien, J. R. R. (John Ronald Reuel), 1892-1973.
Lord of the rings. 2. Fantastic fiction, England—History and criticism.
I. Title.
PR6039.032L635   823'.912   81-12651
ISBN 0-8028-1898-6 (pbk.)   AACR2

CONTENTS

INTRODUCTION

For a number of years I have been wondering why no one wrote this book. Paperback printings of *The Lord of the Rings* number fifty or more. Virtually every bookstore in the United States has a "Tolkien shelf." And certainly numerous books have been written on Tolkien, including the authorized biography by Humphrey Carpenter. And yet (excepting Carpenter's book) I can find no work on Tolkien that gives due weight to the four most obvious facts about the author's life. (Carpenter, who obviously does give consideration to these facts, is, on the other hand, not so much concerned with studying *The Lord of the Rings* as I am here—though I have from time to time quoted from his biography to bolster conclusions I had reached on other grounds. The ideas, if his, are mine also.)

Plainly stated, the four facts are (1) that Tolkien was born on January 3, 1892, and therefore grew to manhood in the years before the Great War; (2) that he was a philologist, winding up as Merton Professor of English Language and Literature in the University of Oxford; (3) that he was a Roman Catholic; and (4) that his magnum opus is one of the most successful works of modern times. In what follows I will use these facts as the basis of my inquiry into *The Lord of the Rings*.

I am emphatically not using Tolkien's work as a key to his character. I am not even (except very briefly in the final chapter) using his character as a key to his work. Either of these might be a worthwhile task—though with C. S. Lewis's disquisition on *The Personal Heresy* in my background I am more than ordinarily skeptical of the first—but neither of them is the task I am undertaking here. What I am hoping to do instead is to ask what kind of work Tolkien intended in *The Lord of the Rings* (and use his Edwardian background as a key); to ask what it is that distinguishes *The Lord of the Rings* from other works in the same genre (and use Tolkien's professional life as a key); to ask in effect what it all means (using, as might be expected, Tolkien's Catholicism as a key); and, finally, to see if these inquiries will reveal what it is about *The Lord of the Rings* that has made it so popular a work.

This approach seems to me self-evident. Certainly I can claim no particular credit for having thought of it. But perhaps the times have not been propitious for any endeavor of this sort until very recently—as a brief review of some critical history may show. For about a dozen years after the book was first published, the three volumes were a kind of underground success, helped by the praise of such reviewers as C. S. Lewis (in England) and W. H. Auden (in the United States), and a few articles in little magazines. One might call this a success of the catacombs, since it was in considerable part a Christian underground. From these dozen years come most of the scholars whose work appears in *Tolkien and the Critics* and *A Tolkien Compass*, as well as some of those, like Clyde Kilby and Paul Kocher, who have written books on Tolkien. But serious criticism of a cult book with limited circulation suffers from what I might here call the *Arthurian Torso* syndrome, after C. S. Lewis's study of Charles Williams. There is nothing quite so likely to leave a critic in an excessively exposed position as an attempt to treat a largely unknown and idiosyncratic work as a major achievement. Thus, from 1954 to 1966 circumstances were not favorable for Tolkien criticism.

Then, in the mid-1960's, when the geyser erupted, the new generation of Tolkien fans, concentrated on college campuses, was not quite the same thing as the old. There were holdovers, of course. The University of Wisconsin Tolkien Society, in those days, included scholars of the old order, aficionados of the new, and some who did not fit neatly into either category. But, by and large, the new enthusiasm was of the sort that plays itself out in fanzines and "looks behind

The Lord of the Rings" and was less likely to produce good literary criticism than the *Arthurian Torso* sort of enthusiasm. For one thing, Tolkien, having passed into popular culture, seemed to be in danger of passing out of the realm of scholarship—except, of course, the scholarship of popular culture. And scholars of popular culture are unlikely to have a background in philology or even in Catholic doctrine; hence the disinclination of scholars (other than scholars from Christian colleges in the American Midwest) to discuss the themes of *The Lord of the Rings*.

The result has been a tendency to talk about Tolkien's work without ever defining what it is—the most obvious and irritating example being the use of the word "trilogy" to describe a six-book, three-decker feigned history that uses the medieval technique of polyphonic narrative to tell what is essentially an adventure story in the Edwardian mode. With so many adjectives or nouns for describing *The Lord of the Rings* more or less accurately, it is symptomatic of a failure in criticism that the one word most widely used is just plain wrong.

Wrong also, in my view, or at least misleading, are a number of other descriptions. Among them, in one respect or another, are "quest" (and this despite Tolkien's own use of the word), "medieval" (except in certain limited ways), and "fantasy" (even in Tolkien's own special sense). Now, since these are, next to "trilogy" (or even, in some contexts, more than "trilogy"), the words most commonly used in connection with *The Lord of the Rings*, it occurs to me that my views may possibly require some justification.

To be sure, there is at least a grain of truth in each description, or the words would not be used as widely as they are. But though the word "quest" in fact appears in *The Lord of the Rings*, the book is not (I would argue) a quest narrative even to the minor degree to which *She* or *King Solomon's Mines* or *The Lost World* are quest narratives. Though the world of *The Lord of the Rings* is medieval in its feel, with its knights and ladies, elves and dwarves, wizards and kings, it is not truly a medieval world: it is virtually without prayer—and besides, if looked at as a medieval world, it shows pronounced anachronisms (Sandyman's new mill, for example, or the entire set of trench-warfare imagery devoted to Mordor). Finally, though "fantasy," especially in Tolkien's definition, seems a word ready-made for *The Lord of the Rings*, the book's Middle Earth is in many ways our familiar world. (This point has been well argued, so far as the return to the Shire is concerned, in an essay by Dr. Robert Plank.)

Even if we were to conclude that *The Lord of the Rings* could reasonably be called a medieval quest fantasy, I do not believe our conclusion would be particularly useful. We have, in general, only a vague and undifferentiated idea what any one of the three words means, and in fact they do not always mean what readers of Tolkien seem to think they do. The model for a "quest" narrative is the *Queste del Sant Graal*, the search for the Holy Grail. "Medieval" refers to a period of time in our own history, characterized by a particular architecture (Gothic), a particular form of art (manuscript illumination), a certain kind of literature (*contes*), a certain kind of society (feudal), and a certain overriding presence (the church). And "fantasy" (to borrow Tolkien's own definition) refers to a form of literary art combining imagination (the mental power of image-making) with unlikeness to the Primary World—that is, with freedom from observed fact. *The Lord of the Rings* is a reverse quest if it is a quest narrative at all: the treasure is to be destroyed, not found. Its Middle Earth is medieval only in its feudal society (even its literature is pre-medieval). And the book is a feigned history of our world. If Tolkien did, in fact, write a fantasy, its name is *Smith of Wootton Major*.

These are not matters central to this book, but I mention them to suggest that my views of Tolkien are to some degree idiosyncratic. To that fact may be traced what some readers will consider an overuse of the first-person singular: I wish to emphasize that what I am saying is my view and not the received or orthodox interpretation. I also wish to give some impression of my own literary travels, both in Tolkien's Middle Earth and in that of such Edwardians as Rider Haggard, Conan Doyle, and the band of scholars who took over Sir James Murray's *New English Dictionary*.

My own travels into Tolkien's world began not with *The Hobbit* or *The Lord of the Rings* but with C. S. Lewis. From the time I first read *Out of the Silent Planet* (in 1951), I had a longing to be part of Ransom's world, and Ransom was a philologist. And from the time I first read *That Hideous Strength* (also in 1951), I longed to read that account of Numinor (so spelled) then existing only "in the MSS of my friend, Professor J. R. R. Tolkien." Thus, when *The Fellowship of the Ring* appeared in 1954, it was on my Christmas list, and I anxiously awaited the conclusion of the story, not published until the next year.

Because Lewis was, as I have argued elsewhere, profoundly influenced by the imaginative life of his friends, and especially by Tolkien's imaginative life, his works provide a legitimate—if dangerous—path on which to approach *The Lord of the Rings*. It is legitimate because of the long and close friendship between the two, which lasted more than a quarter of a century, and because Lewis, a voracious and retentive reader and listener, created his own middle-earth much more from what he read and heard than from what he saw in real life around him. (An exception lies in the brilliant delineation of academic politicking in *That Hideous Strength*, but this need not concern us here.) But this path is dangerous because Tolkien was not the only strong influence on Lewis, and the competing influence, Charles Williams, was unlike Tolkien in almost every way: self-taught, a mystic, a magician, a lover of city pavements, heterodox to Tolkien's orthodoxy, an eccentric, quicksilver, and Renaissance man to Tolkien and his late-nineteenth early-twentieth century centricity. It would be a serious critical error to mistake Lewis-preaching-Williams for Lewis-preaching-Tolkien.

Nevertheless, to approach Tolkien through Lewis is, in general, to approach him from the inside, so to speak—like approaching the English Romantics through Southey or Leigh Hunt. One may go wrong, but one is likely to be going wrong in the right direction. That this is my approach is the result of my own upbringing, and perhaps I should say a few words on that subject here, since I came to Tolkien after a preparation rather different from that of most Tolkien scholars.

The essential characteristic of that preparation was that I grew up on my parents'—and especially my father's—books. That is, I grew up on Conan Doyle (both Sherlock Holmes and Brigadier Gerard, as well as *The White Company* and *Sir Nigel*); on G. A. Henty; on mystery stories (almost all English and including G. K. Chesterton) brought home from the local library in Ho-Ho-Kus, New Jersey; on *The Wind in the Willows* (and, at an earlier age, on *Winnie the Pooh*); and, eventually, on Lewis. There were other books, of course, not so immediately relevant to our concerns here, and there were books at least as relevant that came along later. But these were central, and what was central about them was their Englishness, not in the technical but in the general sense of that word. A child brought up on Peter Wimsey, Reggie Fortune, Sherlock Holmes, and Father Brown is likely to grow into an Anglophile. A child who adds to these the stories of Étienne Gerard, whose humor depends on French misapprehension of the British character, and stories of the days of the Black Prince—and, by the way, Cheyney's *Short History of England*—will have begun to see England as a place apart. Add in a hundred or so books of G. A. Henty's glorification of the British schoolboy, and the mixture is a potent one indeed.

I can say that my experience was like Tolkien's in one respect, at least. I was conscious of England as a separate realm—this *other* Eden, demi-Paradise—to which I was not native but which I ardently desired. I do not suppose this is quite the same feeling as that of the South African-born Tolkien isolated from ordinary English life as an orphan and a Roman Catholic. He was living in the round green land of England but was not of it; I desired it from afar. Yet both experiences, I think, lead to the perception of an ideal England, which is, of course, part of the magic of *The Lord of the Rings*.

I should make one final point. I was raised in a Christian, and specifically a Protestant Episcopal, household, and I attended an Episcopal prep school. Cranmer's cadences in *The Book of Common Prayer* and the rhythms of the King James Version gave me a love of Elizabethan (or Henrician) style. Church music gave me a love of trumpets and voice.

A ceremonial, hierarchical, and sacramental church accustomed me to ceremony, hierarchy, and the use of outward and visible signs for inward and spiritual characteristics. And above and beyond all this, being a Christian tends to lead one to Christian authors and a sympathy for them. That J. R. R. Tolkien was a Christian there has never been any doubt. That he was a Christian author, I hope Chapter III makes clear.

With this background, I find myself attempting this study of *The Lord of the Rings*. In much of what follows I speak with full recognition of the fact that I am suggesting without proof, by indirection, with nothing much to rely on besides my own confidence that I understand *The Lord of the Rings* better than those with whom I disagree—a confidence sometimes shaken and not always a matter of logic. (Note that in what follows I am speaking from *The Lord of the Rings*, not from *The Hobbit*, and especially not from *The Silmarillion*, which would illuminate some of the concerns of Chapter III, at the expense of consistency.)

A shortened form of the first chapter was delivered at the MLA Seminar on Tolkien in New York in December 1976, after being vetted by Christopher Tolkien. I wish to thank him for his courtesy in responding to my requests, Tolkien's publishers for allowing me to quote from *The Lord of the Rings*,* Professor Tolkien himself for his kind responses to my inquiries during his life, Richard West and other members of the University of Wisconsin Tolkien Society, C. S. Lewis for setting me on the road to Tolkien's Middle Earth, and my parents for buying me my first copies of each of the three volumes. None of these is responsible for my views—except, of course, that when these views faithfully interpret Tolkien, the credit is his. In that sense he is responsible for what follows—but only in that sense.

I dedicated an earlier book to Tolkien's followers, wherever and in whatever guise. This one I dedicate to the memory of his predecessors and especially to Sir Henry Rider

---

*Throughout this book I quote from Ballantine editions except as noted.

Haggard: squire of Ditchingham, farmer, lover of England and of far countries, and inventor of the Shard of Amyntas—to which, more than any one thing else, we owe *The Lord of the Rings*.

JARED LOBDELL

Pittsburgh, Pennsylvania
December 1979

CHAPTER I

DEFINING THE LORD OF THE RINGS:
An Adventure Story in the Edwardian Mode

We shall not cease from exploration
And the end of all our exploring
Will be to arrive where we started
And know the place for the first time. . . .
And all shall be well and
All manner of thing shall be well.

T. S. Eliot, ''Little Gidding''

''Beyond the Wild Wood comes the Wide World,'' said the Rat.

Kenneth Grahame, The Wind in the Willows

IT is not at all certain that the game of *Quellenforschung* ("source-hunting") is worth playing with *The Lord of the Rings*, or indeed with most literary creations. Exceptions can be made, of course, for the asking of questions such as "What did Chaucer really do to *Il Filostrato*?" or for the game-playing demanded by *The Waste Land*, but there may well be truth to the suspicion that the game in general is not worth the candle. Yet the search for sources can be part of a search for influences, and the search for influences can be both valid and helpful—as when we look for Vergil's influence on Milton or the influence of the ballads on Coleridge. But we must be looking at both form and subject matter.

Now of course Vergil is an influence on Milton, but is not his source. The influence of the ballads on *The Rime of the Ancient Mariner* is obvious, but it would be a brave man who considered them Coleridge's sources. Nevertheless, if there were a number of secondary epics that might have influenced Milton, we should, I think, be justified in looking to see which of them served as a source, in order to see which was most likely to have served as an influence. Similarly, if we were interested in finding out which ballads influenced Coleridge, we might well look through the ballad corpus for parallels—sources and analogues—for the *Rime*.

This is essentially the kind of endeavor I am engaged in here, for *The Lord of the Rings*. I want to know what kind of work Tolkien set out to write. To which of the great pre-existing forms of literary creation, so different in the expectations they excite and fulfill (the reader may recognize Professor Lewis's words here), so diverse in their powers, is *The Lord of the Rings* designed to contribute? Since we do not have available to us any writings in which Professor Tolkien set down the answer to that question, and since (despite the intentional fallacy) it is indeed "the first qualification for judging any piece of workmanship, from a corkscrew to a cathedral, to know what it is," I think my endeavor is justified. There may of course be better ways than mine to find out what *The Lord of the Rings* is designed to be, but this way seems to be both promising and untrod.

There are two sets of clues to which we should pay particular heed in a search for those whose writing influenced the form of *The Lord of the Rings*, and both sets have been largely overlooked. The first set is composed primarily of Tolkien's own comments and secondarily of those few passages in his work where he obviously echoes another author. The second set is composed of the subjective reactions and literary tastes of those readers of *The Lord of the Rings* who have at least a passing familiarity with the English literature of the period in which Tolkien grew up. The first set of clues provides material for answering the question, "Who, according to what Tolkien wrote, may be considered to have influenced him?" The second provides material for answering the question, "Who wrote the kind of book that affects us in the ways *The Lord of the Rings* affects us and, the dates being right, may therefore have written the kind of book Tolkien would be likely to have read?" (The implicit assumption here is that authors write the kind of book they like to read.)

If we are to make use of both sets of clues, it is of course necessary for us to have some idea of the way Tolkien's mind worked. I suspect there has not been much of value written on this subject, but we can at least make a stab at gaining information sufficient to proceed with our inquiry. We can begin by quoting Tolkien's reaction to the tale of the juniper tree.

"The beauty and horror" of the tale, he says, "with its exquisite and tragic beginning, the abominable cannibal stew, the gruesome bones, the gay and vengeful bird-spirit coming out of a mist that rose from the tree, has remained with me since childhood; and yet always the chief flavour of that tale lingering in the memory was not beauty or horror, but distance and a great abyss of time, not measurable even by *twe tusend Johr*." And, as I hope to demonstrate, we can see in some of Tolkien's other reading the impress of that dark backward and abysm of time. At the same time, we can see in his childhood reading of dictionaries a fascination with languages. Indeed, his mind was chiefly attuned to languages and the past—which is not, I should emphasize, the same thing as being interested in words and history.

I shall have occasion to refer to this again, but it may be a good thing to mention here Tolkien's reference to the remark of Sjera Tomas Saemundsson: "Languages are the chief distinguishing marks of peoples. No people in fact comes into being until it speaks a language of its own; let the languages perish and the peoples perish too, or become different peoples." The languages are more than the words. And, in the same way, the past is more than its history. History is only the facts, or a presentation of the facts, accidentally left to us from the past. We cannot get into the real forest of the past; that is part of what the word "past" means.

It must also be made clear that to give the direction of Tolkien's mind is not yet to explain how his mind worked, only to give what mathematicians might call the parameters of its working. The important thing for us to remember here is that while grammar studies the rules of language, and history studies the rules of the past (one might argue that history is the grammar of the past), Tolkien's reactions to these things were not those of a grammarian. He described *The Lord of the Rings* as containing "in the way of presentation that I find most natural, much of what I personally have received from the study of things Celtic." And he once remarked that "his typical response upon reading a medieval work was to desire not so much to make a philological or critical study of it as to write a modern work in the same tradition."

In Tolkien's professional life the intersection of language and the past came in the realm of philology. In the inward life of his imagination, it came in his creation of a new version of middle-earth. There have, of course, been other versions of middle-earth, from the Midgard of the Norsemen to Langland's fair field full of folk: as Tolkien has reminded us, middle-earth is not his creation, though he created the "Middle Earth" of *The Lord of the Rings*. That act of creation was necessary before a story could be written about his Middle Earth, but it is the story, and not the creation, that is our subject here.

We know that *The Lord of the Rings* was not the first or even the second story whose events took place within the bounds of Tolkien's Middle Earth. It is not even certain it was the third story. We know also that Tolkien wrote other stories as his children were growing up, and it may be that these would repay our attention by giving us additional clues for our endeavor (one of these stories, "Mr Bliss," has been spoken of as "Thurber without the bitterness"). But since we do not have these additional clues, we may reasonably turn to the clues we have, to see where they will lead us.

First, we may look at the writers whose influence Tolkien himself acknowledged, or to whose works he referred, or whose works he conspicuously echoed. The list is not long, and the first name on it, Sir Henry Rider Haggard, is almost certainly the most important. Indeed, in a telephone conversation with the American journalist Henry Resnick, Tolkien said this of Haggard's *She*: "I suppose as a boy *She* interested me as much as anything—like the Greek shard of Amyntas, which was the kind of machine by which everything got moving." And, if that were not enough, we have evident parallels between the death of Ayesha (the She of the title) and the death of Saruman. Perhaps it would be well to set them out here.

Haggard's description of the death of Ayesha may be the less familiar of the two:

> Smaller she grew, and smaller yet, till she was no larger than a monkey. Now the skin had puckered into a million wrinkles, and on her shapeless face was the mark of unutterable age. I never saw anything like it; nobody ever saw anything to equal the infinite age which was graven on that fearful countenance, no bigger now than that of a two-months' child, though the skull retained its same size. . . . I took up Ayesha's kirtle and the gauzy scarf . . . and, averting my head so that I might not look upon it, I covered up that dreadful relic (Dover ed., pp. 222-223).

Beside this may be set Tolkien's description of the death of Saruman:

> Frodo looked down on the body with pity and horror, for as he looked it seemed that long years of death were suddenly revealed in it, and it shrank, and the shrivelled face became rags of skin upon a hideous skull. Lifting up the skirt of the dirty cloak that sprawled beside it, he covered it over, and turned away (III, 370).

The parallel is not exact, but it is certainly highly suggestive. Nor do I think I would be stretching a point to bring in, as additional evidence, the predominant importance of caves in both Haggard and Tolkien. In *King Solomon's Mines*, the Don is found dead in a cave on the way, the dead kings are enthroned in the cave, and the travelers are very nearly entombed there as well. In *She* the secret fire of immortality, which destroys Ayesha, is likewise in a cave— and, of course, both fire and cave have their parallels in Orodruin. And Moria, Shelob's lair—all those dark places where "the flowers of symbelmynë come never to the world's end"—testify eloquently to what is at least a noteworthy similarity between the two. (Freudians may find a different explanation; I prefer mine.)

Perhaps it would also be worth recalling here that Haggard was drawn to Africa, where he had been secretary to the Governor of Natal, because of its mystery, its age-old past, and even (though not so strongly) the majesty of its languages. Given this evidence, I think we will not be far wrong if we assign to Haggard a chief place among Tolkien's literary forebears.

Next among them—and here we may be on more tenuous grounds—we find G. K. Chesterton, between whose works and Tolkien's "On Fairy Stories" we can trace a set of connections, including some Tolkienian passages with a remarkably Chestertonian ring. Let me give you some examples of what I mean. Andrew Lang once remarked that the taste of children "remains like the taste of their naked ancestors thousands of years ago." Tolkien began his response by saying, "But do we really know much about these 'naked ances-

tors' except that they were certainly not naked?" When Max
Muller claimed that mythology was a "disease of language,"
Tolkien made this reply:

> Mythology is not a disease at all, though it may like all
> human things become diseased. You might as well say
> that thinking is a disease of the mind. It would be more
> near the truth to say that languages, especially modern
> European languages, are a disease of mythology.

Either response could have been written by Chesterton, and
the first, in fact, echoes a passage in *The Everlasting Man*.

Finally, I would challenge readers who do not recognize
it to tell me whether Tolkien or Chesterton wrote the passage
which is my third example:

> We may put a deadly green upon a man's face and
> produce a horror; we may make the rare and terrible
> blue moon to shine; or we may cause woods to spring
> with silver leaves and rams to wear fleeces of gold, and
> put hot fire into the belly of the cold worm.

In fact, the quotations are from "On Fairy Stories" (from the
Tolkien Reader, Ballantine, pp. 62, 48, 49). Nevertheless, we
do not know whether Tolkien read the early Chesterton of
The Man Who Was Thursday or *The Napoleon of Notting Hill*.
On the available evidence we can only say that it seems
highly likely, and on that basis look briefly at what Chesterton
was trying to do, and what it was that he succeeded in doing.

Haggard in ordinary life was a sufficiently prosaic En-
glishman (an expert on English agriculture) and sought in his
books to portray the romance of what everyone could see
was romantic. Chesterton, on the other hand, was anything
but ordinary (witness the fictional portrait in John Dickson
Carr's Gideon Fell), and I think it not coincidental that he
sought to portray the romance of what everyone could see
was prosaic: "We feel it is epical when man with one wild
arrow strikes a distant bird. Is it not also epical when man
with one wild engine strikes a distant station?" It is true that
Chestertonian paradox can grow wearying, but the root of
his love for paradox lies in the not at all paradoxical belief

that the wide world is really a remarkably interesting place after all.

How, then, might this have influenced Tolkien in *The Lord of the Rings*? Most directly, I believe, in the very character of the Hobbits. As Chesterton's Father Brown is short and round and the essence of the Norfolk flats, so Bilbo Baggins is short and round and the essence of an English shire. Perhaps the Battle of Bywater is not unlike the battles in *The Napoleon of Notting Hill*. Of course, at these points Chestertonian paradox was touching something deep in the paradoxical character of England, and Tolkien could certainly have touched it entirely without Chesterton's intermediation. But I do not think he did.

Third among the authors Tolkien read—and here I claim an unfair advantage in the game of *Quellenforschung*—was Algernon Blackwood. The evidence I have seen lies in an entry in the original (but not the edited and published) version of the "Notes on the Nomenclature of *The Lord of the Rings*," in which Tolkien traces his use of "the crack of doom" to an unidentified story by Blackwood. Now for our purposes it is unimportant whether the source of Tolkien's Crack of Doom (in Orodruin) was indeed something Blackwood wrote; what is important is that Tolkien could not have thought it was if he had not read (and been influenced by) Blackwood. I suspect there may be confirmatory evidence for the reading (and the influence) in the character of Old Man Willow, though he is not so terrible as the willows in Blackwood's story of that name.

Blackwood's narrator writes of the "acres of willows, crowding ... pressing upon the river as though to suffocate it, standing in dense array mile after mile beneath the sky, watching, waiting, listening. ... Their serried ranks, growing everywhere darker about me as the shadows deepened ... woke in me the curious and unwelcome suggestion that we had trespassed here upon the borders of ... a world where we were intruders, a world where we were not invited to remain." And a little later "the note of this willow-camp became unmistakably plain to me: we were interlopers, trespassers; we were not wanted. The sense of unfamiliarity grew

upon me." And finally (in a passage with Entish—or perhaps
Huornish—connotations), "They first became visible, these
huge figures, just within the tops of the bushes—immense,
bronze-coloured, moving. . . . I saw them plainly and noted,
now I came to examine them more calmly, that they were
very much larger than human, and indeed that something
in their appearance proclaimed them to be *not human* at all.
. . . I saw their limbs and huge bodies . . . rising up in a living
column . . ." (*Strange Stories*, Heinemann ed., pp. 635-6, 644,
647).

The style is different, of course, and yet I catch in Blackwood something I catch in Tolkien but in few others—perhaps at night in the wildwood in *The Wind in the Willows*
also (yet those willows are friendlier). I mean a sense of man
(or Hobbit) as interloper in the woods, of the trees as sentient
entities, and of something neither tree nor human—nor yet,
as with Saki, clearly Pan. And in the same volume ("The Glam-
our of the Snow" in *Strange Stories*) I find passages (on pages
125 and 127) that could be glosses on the experience with
Caradhras.

Here the hero of the story (not the same as in "The
Willows") "tried to turn away in escape, and so trying, found
for the first time that the power of the snow—that other
power which does not exhilarate but deadens effort—was
upon him. The suffocating weakness that it brings to ex-
hausted men, luring them to the sleep of death in her cling-
ing soft embrace, lulling the will and conquering all desire
for life—this was awfully upon him." And then, as he es-
capes, "For ever close upon his heels came the following
forms and voices with the whirling snow-dust. He heard that
little silvery voice of death and laughter at his back. Shrill
and wild, with the whistling of the wind past his ears, he
caught its pursuing tones; but in anger now. . . ."

I am not suggesting here that Blackwood is Tolkien's
source for the character of Old Man Willow or for the snow-
storm at Caradhras; he could be, I suppose, but it is not in
this that his importance lies. What I am suggesting is that
the cast of Blackwood's mind, as revealed in these passages,
is surprisingly like the cast of Tolkien's mind. It does not

much matter whether the snow at Caradhras comes from Tolkien's alpine experiences or from Blackwood's. It matters considerably that they saw the snow in much the same way.

Indeed, it matters enough that we should ask what Blackwood was doing in his stories. The answer is that he was creating the modern story of the supernatural—not the pure ghost story of M. R. James or the story of the un-dead that found its best-known expression in Bram Stoker's *Dracula*, but the story in which (if I may be forgiven a paradox of my own) nature itself is in a way supernatural. To be sure, Blackwood wrote ghost stories and stories of the un-dead, and he wrote stories that did not concern the supernatural at all, but what he added to English literature was a sense of mystery and unreliability underlying ordinary things. Blackwood's vision was of the treachery of natural things in an animate world: call it their mystery if you will, but the mystery has a sinister touch.

It is hard for us to re-create any world-view, especially the view of a world in which we have not lived, but there is little doubt that the generations of England who were brought up on Haggard, on Chesterton, on Blackwood—and on Stevenson, Conan Doyle, G. A. Henty, even Saki—were brought up as romantics, in the common sense of that word. While it is not easy to define romanticism in that common sense, we may at least note that ghost stories and stories of the un-dead make their first appearance in modern English literature with the Romantics, unless of course one wishes to count *Hamlet* as a ghost story. In any case, that these generations, and their romanticism, died in the trenches of the Great War is a truism. Like other truisms it is both true and overlooked, as it seems to be overlooked that Tolkien fought in that war and began his first epic of Middle Earth while convalescing.

It should be emphasized that the Edwardians of whom I am speaking were all of them storytellers. Their poetry— one thinks of Masefield or Kipling—was narrative poetry, even if it was not a narrative of princes and prelates. To a greater extent than in most of Victoria's reign, their natural form of narrative was the short story (it is worth recalling that only by an exercise of almost undiluted romanticism did Conan Doyle, in *The Hound of the Baskervilles*, succeed in writing a satisfactory novel about Sherlock Holmes). But their short stories in many cases, and their novels in some, were installments in a continuing story. I have elsewhere called these Edwardians "world-creators," and I am not sure how important it is that their worlds were created monthly in *The Strand* rather than in the three-deckers of Trollope's age. After all, Dickens published his novels in parts, but they are still novels, and (witness the Baker Street Irregulars) the world of Sherlock Holmes is still one world for all that it was created story by story over the years. The important point is that what were being told were stories—not tone-poems, not Dunsanian lyrics, not Mervyn Peake's word-pictures (though they may be first-rate of their kind), but stories.

All this should give an idea, albeit a sketchy one, of what kind of information exists to make up our first set of clues. It must be admitted that the information is not abundant. We have Tolkien's own word for it that he was neither as voracious nor as retentive a reader as his friend Lewis, and of course Lewis wrote that "no one ever influenced Tolkien—you might as well try to influence a bandersnatch." (Someone more adept than I at the intricacies of Carrolliana may know why a bandersnatch would be particularly difficult to influence.) Even so, no writer, when young, is immune to influences, and it is certainly reasonable for us to use such clues as we have to try to determine who Tolkien's influences were.

Our second set of clues is, alas, equally sparse. One reason is that critics in general (despite Lewis's lead in his *Experiment in Criticism*) have not addressed themselves to most works of literature with the question in mind, "How is this book being read?" Another reason, at least as important, is that criticism of Tolkien has generally begun *de novo* with Tolkien, just as most criticism of science fiction seems to begin *de novo* with the field of science fiction, as though no other fiction had ever been written. But to this approach to Tolkien *de novo* there are at least two exceptions that may be of use in our inquiry, both of them provided by English critics. The particular writers they pick as Tolkien's compeers are not, as it happens, the ones I would pick, but this may only mean that their taste in Edwardian literature differs from mine. Even if they are not entirely on the right track, I am convinced at least that the track they are on begins from the right place.

Mr. Colin Wilson suggests a relationship between Tolkien and Jeffrey Farnol. Now to say that Jeffrey Farnol is widely overlooked in histories of English literature is to overstate the notice taken of him, but as Mr. Wilson points out, his picaresque novels were enthusiastically circulated among the members of Tolkien's generation. I do not myself believe that Tolkien read the novels of Jeffrey Farnol, but I emphatically do believe that Mr. Wilson reads Farnol's novels and Tolkien's three-decker for much the same reasons.

Similarly, Mr. Brian Aldiss compares Tolkien to the late P. G. Wodehouse. Now this is curious. Mr. Aldiss is a scholar of science fiction and fantasy, and his discussion of Tolkien occurs in his history of science fiction. Yet for a comparison he goes to an author who did not write science fiction (though he may have written fantasy), and who would not generally be considered to place high on the list of "authors comparable to Tolkien." Upon consideration, I can see more reasons than were initially apparent for the comparison—Wodehouse was, after all, a world-creator, and of a very English world at that—but linking the two still has a certain oddness to it. Oddness aside, it provides us with the evidence that Mr. Aldiss reads Tolkien at least for some of the reasons he reads Wodehouse.

My own contribution here may be at least as odd. I might reasonably make a general case for the parallel between Tolkienian "scholarship" and the "scholarship" devoted to the arcana of Sherlock Holmes—thus suggesting that some readers turn to Tolkien for the same reason that others turn to 221B Baker Street. I have already discussed the parallels between Tolkien and Rider Haggard, and could easily claim I read one for largely the same reasons I read the other. But I find by self-analysis that—in some moods at least—I read Tolkien as I read Saki (H. H. Munro).

That is a fact. What to do with it is a problem. Presumably I should be able to find an undercurrent of Tolkien's vision in Saki or an undercurrent of Saki's vision in Tolkien, or else find that I am particularly attracted to the Edwardian world-view exemplified by both. For the first, I cannot imagine that Tolkien enjoyed Saki: their humor, if not poles apart, is at least extremely dissimilar, and Tolkien lacks Saki's cruelty. Certainly any connection between Frodo Baggins and Clovis Sangrail is not obvious, nor—to put it mildly—is Comus Bassington the avatar of Gandalf the Grey. Admittedly, both Saki and Tolkien were Tories, and my own mind has that cast, but I would prefer for the moment to leave that line of thought aside as a possible red herring (or perhaps, in the circumstances, a blue herring?). I suspect that my turning to Saki, Mr. Aldiss's turning to Wodehouse, and Mr. Wilson's turning to Jeffrey Farnol have in common principally the fact that each of us is turning to the first (or close to the first) Edwardian author with whom we came in contact. I should note here that Mr. William Ready has observed the Edwardian nature of *The Lord of the Rings*, but he shuns what I welcome. Still, this is useful confirmatory evidence.

Those who have followed me thus far may think it odd, if not remarkable, that I have managed to discuss the sources and analogues of *The Lord of the Rings* without turning to the *Elder Edda* or *Beowulf* or any of the other commonplaces of the discussions generally heard on the literary genesis of Tolkien's work. But those are properly the subject of another inquiry: they are part of the influence of Tolkien's professional life on his imaginative life (though not the most important part). This, by contrast, is a look at the influence of other imaginative writers on Tolkien's imaginative life, so far as that influence affects the form of his work. By the nature of things (at least according to the "bandersnatch" theory), the *terminus ad quem* of this inquiry more or less antedates the *terminus a quo* of the other.

I have noted Tolkien's statement that his first response on reading a medieval work was to want to write a modern work in the same tradition. If that was true throughout his life, and not only of medieval works, then it is certainly proper to look at the kind of stories he read to see what kind of stories he was trying to write. I could wish I had in front of me the earliest manuscript of *The Silmarillion* as a check on my speculation, but failing that I have *The Lord of the Rings*, as well as a set of clues on the authors Tolkien read, and a set of clues made up of readers' reactions to Tolkien.

From these clues I would argue, with some confidence, that in *The Lord of the Rings* Tolkien set out to write an adventure story of the Rider Haggard sort, with overtones of G. K. Chesterton and undertones of Algernon Blackwood (to take only the authors mentioned here), an adventure story in what may be called the Edwardian mode. I would like to argue—anticlimax or not—that this "adventure story in the Edwardian mode" was precisely a "pre-existing form of literary creation" with its own set of expectations to excite and fulfill, and its own diverse powers. And I would like to spend some time examining the form.

The Edwardian adventure story might be of the "I have before me as I write" sort (to borrow Peter Fleming's phrase), in which a particular object associated with the adventure leads the author into his book. It might be a fictional travelogue, or at least a travel story, beginning with some such phrase as "It's eighteen months or so ago since I first met Sir Henry Curtis and Captain Good, and it was in this way." But however the story began, in general it would, like Conan Doyle's *The Lost World*, be framed in familiarity.

This is, in many ways, the mode of the fairy tale, though we do not always recognize it because the woodchoppers and petty kings with which the tales begin are, as Professor Lewis pointed out, as remote to us as the dragons and witches to which the tales proceed. But this is not quite the mode of the fairy tale, for the fairy tale begins "once upon a time," while the Edwardian adventure story begins in rooms in Oxford in the late 1880's, or rooms in Baker Street in the same decade, or with a Fleet Street journalist's assignment to interview an eccentric professor, or with an English poet in Saffron Park in the London of the Edwardian age. In economist's jargon, these beginnings are "time-specific."

In this adventure story odd and inexplicable things

happen, not in Oxford or Baker Street or Saffron Park, but in the land of the Amahagger, or on Dartmoor, or on a lost plateau in South America, or in a kaleidoscopic adventure across a Europe of enchanted scenery and stock characters—the Europe, one might say, of a dream. In no case is characterization the chief concern of the story. Holly and Job in *She*, Malone and Lord John and Summerlee in *The Lost World*, Holmes and Watson themselves, the Council of Days in *The Man Who Was Thursday*—all are types: the "true but ugly," the "faithful servant," and so on. That they sometimes, as with Holmes, rise to the dignity of archetypes takes them further yet from the novel of character.

In a sense, even if it is a paradoxical sense, in many of these stories it is the character of nature, and not the characters of any of the actors, that is, as the French would put it, "realized." That is why Blackwood's "The Willows" follows naturally in the Edwardian mode: there is no real effort at characterization (the author's companion is a stolid Scandinavian), except at the characterization of the willows themselves. And the character that nature bears in these stories is not altogether a good one. (I suspect, by way of personal aside, that this is one of the attributes of Saki's work that appeals to me: there is a fey quality to "The Hounds of Fate" and "The Stag" and a thoroughgoing supernaturalism to "Gabriel-Ernest," standing in remarkable contrast to the world of Reginald or Clovis Sangrail. For comparison one might look to Badger's house on the one hand, and the Piper at the Gates of Dawn on the other.)

It should particularly be noted that the adventurers in the Edwardian adventure story are, in general, not solitary. They may indeed be "we few, we happy few," but (if only so that one may tell the story of the others), they are at least two in number—Holmes and Watson, for example. They are likely to be more than two: indeed, the characteristic Edwardian adventure story is that of Sir Henry Curtis, Captain Good, Allan Quatermain, and Ignosi, or of G. E. Challenger, Lord John Roxton, Edward Malone, and Professor Summerlee—the band of (very different) brothers. And the narrative is in the first person, even if it involves that first person's bringing in parts of the story of which he had no firsthand knowledge. That is, there is a convention that the story should be told by those whose story it is. In general, the narrator is the most ordinary member of the band of adventurers (Allan Quatermain, Edward Malone, John Watson), and the tone of the narration tends to be self-depreciating.

This tone, and the first-person narration, mark the Edwardian mode as something quite apart from the mode of the fairy tale or (*pace* Edmund Wilson) from the school story—though the school story does perhaps represent a separate but related development from the Victorians. I suppose this Edwardian mode of the adventure story had its origin in the travel journals and first-person newspaper accounts that were conspicuous features of the English and American literary landscape in the second half of the nineteenth century. The names of Richard Burton and H. M. Stanley come immediately to mind, followed by the war correspondent W. H. Russell and the American John Lloyd Stephens, whose *Incidents of Travel in Central America, Chiapas, and Yucatan* is one of the finest examples of this Victorian literature of exploration. It should, however, be pointed out that the self-depreciating tone comes in later, and may have its origins in the tradition of the *pukka sahib*—stiff upper lip, British understatement, and all that—that is in part the legacy of the Duke of Wellington. In any event, the Edwardian adventure story would appear to be a case of art imitating life.

One could, I suppose, distinguish between this travel literature and the derivative literature of Rider Haggard or Conan Doyle, on the grounds that one is more interested in the traveling and the other in what lies at the end—the object of the quest—thus making *King Solomon's Mines* or *She* into a quest story. But I am not sure this would be profitable. The Edwardian adventure story was indeed a story of Englishmen abroad in the wide and mysterious world, but what they were looking for was not so much the Holy Grail or the Golden Fleece as—whatever excuse may have been provided by Maple White or the Shard of Amyntas—the wide world itself. (It is worth noting that the best of Blackwood's stories take place on the Danube or in Canada or in the Alps.) And

I find this parallels *The Lord of the Rings*: it does not seem to me that Frodo sets out on a quest much more than Bilbo set out on one in *The Hobbit*. Certainly Frodo and Bilbo, though they are Hobbits, are Englishmen, and to them the "back again" in the subtitle of *The Hobbit* is as important as the "there."

As I have said, the actors in these Edwardian stories were stock Englishmen, most of them. Mostly they returned to England and their workaday lives, if they survived at all. It is not my purpose here to point out in detail how *The Lord of the Rings* conforms to the Edwardian mode, only to suggest its conformity, but perhaps another example of that mode would not be amiss. The example that comes most quickly to mind (though it is late, having appeared in 1923) is John Buchan's *Huntingtower*, in which the character of the Scottish businessman is so Tolkienian that one would almost assume that Tolkien took time off from *The Year's Work in English Studies* to read Buchan. Buchan, admittedly, was Scottish, while the Shire is "forever England"—but that is not an insuperable difference.

The quite ordinary Englishmen (or, occasionally, Scots or Irishmen) who set off on their travels in these Edwardian adventure stories do more than merely see strange sights and have strange adventures: they sense a mysterious character indwelling in the world itself, or at least in that part of the world in which the adventures take place. The story may be of their triumph over nature (as with *The Lost World*), or it may be of their escape from it ("The Willows"). It may be, in its later and lesser form, a story of romance and a mysterious Russian princess (as with *Huntingtower*). Or the mystery may be—and frequently is—that of the past mysteriously alive in the present. This is the case with *King Solomon's Mines*, *She*, *The Lost World*, much of Chesterton, and the very idea of the ghost story, whether by Blackwood or M. R. James or whomever. In fact, from the number of examples I can call to mind, this might be taken as a hallmark of the Edwardian mode. To be sure, others have felt the lure of the past: it is a part of the nature of romanticism, and it was a Victorian, not an Edwardian, who wrote (if he wrote nothing else worthwhile) the great line "A rose red city half as old as time." But the past alive in the present is a recurring motif in the Edwardian adventure story nonetheless.

The framework of the story, even in Haggard's time, is "there and back again." The "back again" is skimped, and it would appear, in part, a convention necessitated by the first-person narrative: the narrator has to return home in order to tell his story (though Haggard did find a way around this in *She*). By Blackwood's time—as a result, I suppose, of the short-story form—the framework largely disappears, and we are left with the real kernel of the story, which in Blackwood is the mystery (or the "supernaturalism") of nature. (Chesterton dropped the first-person narrative, while retaining the viewpoint of the first-person narrator, who likewise must return home to tell the story.)

It may be objected that I have taken three disparate authors and parceled them together very oddly, and that an "Edwardian mode" that overlooks Baron Corvo on the one hand or Henry James on the other is scarcely worth discussing seriously. Now I could look at either of these and find something of the sense of the past I have been discussing here, just as I could find it in Bram Stoker. But what have I, and what has Tolkien, to do with feigned autobiography in the manner of *Hadrian VII* or novels of character in the manner of *The Ambassadors*? The ancestry of the adventure story in its Edwardian mode is to be found in Scott and the Dickens of *A Tale of Two Cities*, as well as in Burton, Stanley, John Lloyd Stephens—the list is almost endless. It has its late Victorian affinities in G. A. Henty—and as in Henty's novels, where boys who make their way without benefit of birth are frequently found to have had that benefit all along (but to have been stolen or orphaned as very young children), the Edwardian adventure story is frankly aristocratic in its conventions, as was the Edwardian world from which it came.

That *The Lord of the Rings* is an exemplar of this Edwardian mode is at the root of the adverse reactions by such readers as William Ready or Edmund Wilson. In a way—and here Mr. Aldiss is quite correct—its basic presuppositions are those of P. G. Wodehouse, though Tolkien's knowledge of

political reality was far superior to Wodehouse's (on which
see Dr. Plank's essay on "The Scouring of the Shire"). I am
not here concerned with the literary value of Edwardian adventure stories (except to note that Lewis's test in his *Experiment in Criticism* should convince us that they have a
value). But Tolkien's adverse critics have in fact been concerned with that value, to the extent of denying that it exists.
I am not here concerned with such questions as whether
the aristocratic—or the Tory—view of things is the right one.
But Tolkien's adverse critics have in fact been concerned with
that question, and have come up with an unequivocal answer, unequivocally expressed. What the adverse critics have
not been concerned with is what I am concerned with here:
using my scattered evidence on sources to find out what
kind of work Tolkien is likely to have been writing.

Certainly this adventure story in the Edwardian mode
is a prime candidate to be considered the pre-existing form
to which *The Lord of the Rings* was designed to contribute.
At the very least, a formal comparison of *The Lord of the
Rings* with various exemplars of the mode should prove to
be enlightening. While not making the formal comparison
here, I might suggest the lines along which it could be made.
Take Conan Doyle's *The Lost World* as an exemplar. In this
story the four travelers come together more or less by accident—or by the machinations of Professor Challenger (who
is not with them for the entire journey). *The Lord of the Rings*
has, of course, nine travelers, who come together more or
less by accident—or partly by Gandalf's intent (and Gandalf
does not make the entire journey with them). The four travel
to unknown lands, seeking a way up (and then a way down)
a mysterious plateau—involving, on the way down, travel
through a cave. The Nine Walkers likewise travel to unknown
lands, with Frodo and Sam seeking a way up (through Shelob's cave). The four are types: sportsman, Irish rugger, des-
iccated (but tough) professor, eccentric omnicompetent. The
Nine likewise are types: master and man, enthusiastic but
fallible assistants, warrior, king-in-exile, elf, dwarf, and the
eccentric omnicompetent, Gandalf.

Further parallels are easy enough to discover. Nature—

in the form of prehistoric animals and even (perhaps) the ape-men—attacks the four. Nature—in the form of Old Man Willow or the snow at Caradhras—attacks the Nine. The four come safely through to the triumph; eight of the Nine Walkers do likewise. The story of the four is told by the most "ordinary" of the group, Edward Dunn Malone (but, ordinary or not, "there are heroisms all around us"). Similarly, the story of the Nine is told by Frodo, whom David Miller has called "the common lens for heroic experience"—ordinary on the surface if not beneath it. The very attraction of the lost world is the past alive in the present on the mysterious plateau. And certainly the continually sounding theme of *The Lord of the Rings* is the past alive in the present: the Ring, Gandalf, Galadriel, Elrond, the sword reforged, the Barrow Wights—to list examples is to list nearly everything in the book.

I have elsewhere suggested that after the Great War there was a division in the Edwardian inheritance between the storytellers and the world-recreators—between Edgar Rice Burroughs and Angela Thirkell, the pulp writers and the country-house novelists. One might almost say the division was between those who were chiefly interested in the "there" and those who were chiefly interested in the "back again." I still think that this is true, and that, as I also suggested, Tolkien brought the long-sundered branches of the Edwardian line back together again—for which reason he, more than P. G. Wodehouse, deserved the title of "the last Edwardian." But I am not sure how much emphasis this merits here. Though the Shire's Tory quality is unmistakable, its idylls include no country houses, and my present concern is not with the Edwardian inheritance so much as the Edwardian mode of *The Lord of the Rings*—with the fact that, whatever the mode in which others were writing, Tolkien was writing an Edwardian adventure story.

It may be introduced as an objection that the Edwardian mode tended at least toward shorter novels, and in its final form toward the short story. Moreover, the speed of its writing, as well as the pace of its action, was almost journalistic. Haggard wrote *King Solomon's Mines* in six weeks,

and Conan Doyle cranked out Sherlock Holmes at high speed
for monthly publication. Chesterton wrote prodigiously, hastily—one might say, gargantuanly. But Tolkien wrote a three-
decker novel and he took forty years to write it, if one counts
from his beginning *The Silmarillion*, or twenty-five years, if
one counts from the time he began the story of Bilbo Baggins.
I think we will find, however, that the variation in the basic
form represented by *The Lord of the Rings* was determined
by Tolkien's professional life, and its period of gestation determined the same way. That is to say, what differentiates
Tolkien from other writers of Edwardian adventure stories
generally would be properly treated in a discussion of the
influence of his professional life on his imaginative creation,
with the root of the difference lying in the love of language
that led him to philology as his life's work.

But that, as Aristotle taught us the formula (long before
Kipling), is another story. To be exact, it is the story of the
philologist's world, and not the Edwardian mode, of *The
Lord of the Rings*. To write it requires some knowledge of
what a philologist does and how his mind works. To write
what I have written here so far has required only a knowledge of what it was Tolkien read in the first ten years of this
century, or may have read—a far easier requirement, and
made easier yet for me by the fact that I was brought up on
the same books. To me this game of *Quellenforschung* has
been a game of auld acquaintance, and doubly enjoyable on
that account.

But it has been, I hope, instructive to the reader besides
being entertaining to me. And its value, I think, is clear: we
will be armed against a tendency to attack (or defend) Tolkien
on the wrong grounds if we can determine what the proper
grounds are—that is, what *The Lord of the Rings* is intended
to be. To go back for a moment to Professor Lewis's example,
it is necessary to know what the corkscrew or the cathedral
is designed to do before we can say it is well- or ill-designed:
once we know what the purposes are, the prohibitionist may
attack the corkscrew or the Communist attack the cathedral.
And here it is important that we realize one thing: the attack
of the prohibitionist or the Communist is not an attack on

how well the corkscrew or the cathedral works. The better the corkscrew works, the less the prohibitionist will like it. The more men pray in the cathedral, the more the Communist will seek to shut it down. The greater the success of *The Lord of the Rings* as an adventure story in the Edwardian mode, the more those who dislike adventure stories in the Edwardian mode will seek to denigrate and depreciate it.

In part, the critical dislike of this mode is merely an example of the critical dislike of adventure stories of all kinds, a point which Professor Lewis illustrated in his essay "On Stories" and which I need not illustrate here. But the dislike runs deeper for this mode than for others, and I suspect that there are those who enjoy *Don Quixote* or *The Three Musketeers* who do not enjoy the Edwardian adventure story any more than they enjoy the *Chanson de Roland*, with its good Christians and bad infidels ("Paiens ont tort et chrestiens ont droit"). The different modes of the adventure story appeal, I believe, to somewhat different—perhaps very different— audiences, and it would be a mistake not to distinguish among these modes.

The particular characteristics of the Edwardian mode that seem to cause the most trouble for the critics are those that apparently form the substratum of almost all popular Edwardian literature: the aristocratic view, the black-and-white morality, the lack of interest in character development (certainly more extreme in this mode than in others), the movement of "there and back again," the emphasis on "we few, we happy few" (related to, but not altogether the same as, the aristocratic view), the fascination of the past alive in the present, the undercurrent of mystery (or even malignity) in nature. If one looks at the chief forms of the adventure story a few years into the last quarter of the twentieth century, he will find not these but the morally ambiguous: the hard-drinking and hard-wenching private eye, the solipsistic James Bond, the not-so-good sheriff and not-so-bad outlaw. If all these are part of the current mode of the adventure story, we could reasonably expect to find the Edwardian mode disliked.

Now the evidence of Mr. Wilson and Mr. Aldiss (and in

conversation I have found others who support his linking of
Tolkien and Wodehouse), as well as my own aberration in
the direction of the world of Clovis Sangrail, should make it
clear that there are some readers who enjoy the Edwardian
character of *The Lord of the Rings*, for all that Mr. Wilson
seems a little uncomfortable in his position and Mr. Aldiss
speaks of "the counterfeit gold of an Edwardian sunset." But
we must be careful not to claim greatness for Tolkien merely
because we are enamored of the Edwardian mode, just as
those who dislike it should be careful not to deny him greatness because they are not so enamored.

And yet, I can hear my readers saying to themselves,
"This is all very well, but how can he speak of the Edwardian
mode of the adventure story in the same terms in which
Lewis spoke of something so far beyond it as the secondary
epic? Surely it is a little odd to speak of Tolkien in terms that
have been reserved for Vergil or Milton. Surely he has lost his
sense of proportion." But a brief explanation should allay
such misgivings.

It may indeed be the case that an epic is a greater thing
than an adventure story; that does not mean that a given
epic is greater than a given adventure story. I could also point
out that Milton's "Epic following Nature" is very like an adventure story—perhaps, indeed, it would be well to note this
as a corrective to the view that an adventure story is an
inferior thing. Moreover, if a critical system is well drawn up,
it should be applicable not only to Vergil and Milton but to
the writers of three-deckers (let us say Tolkien and Trollope)
as well. And there remains the corrective supplied in Professor Lewis's *Experiment*: if the work is capable of "good" reading (and especially of re-reading), then we had best be wary
of dismissing it out of hand, or indeed at all. After all, popular
literature (*vide* Shakespeare in his age) is not necessarily bad,
and there is a genuine critical approach embodied in the
assertion, "I don't know much about art but I know what I
like."

Admittedly, we are too close in time to *The Lord of the
Rings* to judge its place in literary history. Yet we are not
close enough in time, it appears, to judge accurately what

it is supposed to be. Tolkien disliked the idea that anyone might write a critical study of his work while he was alive, both because he was a private man not welcoming fame and because he thought it wrong that someone should spin theories about what he had written without checking those theories with him. One appreciates his point, but one must also recognize that it has made criticism of his work more difficult: just as one would have enjoyed a talk with Lewis's ancient Athenian, if not his dinosaur in the laboratory, one would like to have spoken with the last Edwardian.

I suspect more may be recovered than I have recovered here. Haggard and Chesterton and Blackwood were not the only authors the young Tolkien read, and Mr. Wilson and Mr. Aldiss are certainly not the only critics to have examined Tolkien's work in ways that are useful for this kind of endeavor. But I would strongly urge those who seek more information to follow this path. Certainly enough evidence exists to show that *The Lord of the Rings* is an adventure story in the Edwardian mode. And whether we believe it to be as sublime as the cathedral, or as mundane as the corkscrew, or somewhere in between in merry middle-earth, it should be worth something to us to have some idea what it is.

CHAPTER II

THE PHILOLOGIST'S WORLD OF THE LORD OF THE RINGS

By the delicate, invisible web you wove —
The inexplicable mystery of sound.

T. S. Eliot, "To Walter de la Mare"

Bright is the ring of words
When the right man rings them.

Robert Louis Stevenson, "If This Were Faith"

TOLKIEN began work on *The Silmarillion* while recovering from the trench fever he contracted during the Great War. But he first achieved prose publication in quite a different genre (if indeed "prose" and "genre" are the right words here): in his glossary of Middle English published in 1922, and in his reports on current scholarship for *The Year's Work in English Studies* in the years immediately following. To these may be added his work on the *New English Dictionary* (now better known as the *OED*) in 1919-1920. The founder of that great achievement, Sir James Murray, had died a few years before, his work unfinished but his goal in sight—a complete dictionary of the English tongue on historical principles, following each word in all its changes through time, from the time of its first recorded usage to the present day (or, in this case, the 1920's). Tolkien was one of the young scholars appointed to finish the task in the years after the War.

It probably need not be pointed out here that the construction of a dictionary on historical principles is a scholarly version of the effort to see (or define) the past alive in the present. What may need to be pointed out is the immensity of the task that James Murray set for himself (and, much later, his assistants). It took almost six decades from beginning to end (if, indeed, it has ended yet), and six decades was a short time for what was accomplished.

But calling attention to its immensity is paying only half the tribute due. The long unfolding of the English language from *Beowulf* (or even before) to the present day is a great story. The whole panoply of the Indo-European tongues, spread out through space and time over the whole world and six millennia, is one of the greatest stories ever told. And Murray—and those who came after—were caught up in its greatness.

Languages, of course, obey certain laws defining or describing their modification over time, and they obey these laws, generally speaking, in all times and all places, regardless of the separate genius of the language. Whether it is *holbytla* becoming *hobbit* or *kud-dukan* becoming *kuduk* (to take examples from *The Lord of the Rings*), whether it is *per-awa-mes-enki* becoming *peramessing* and then *paramus* (this is Algonquian) or *generalis* (Latin) becoming *geral* (Portuguese), the words wear down. So, too, does the structure of the languages. They begin by being highly inflected—verbs with different forms for each person of a whole array of moods and tenses, nouns with different forms for each of many numbers and cases. African tribes count "one - two - three - many" (which sounds simple), and have a different form of the noun involved for each of the four numbers (which is not simple at all). Latin preserves seven different cases—nominative, accusative, genitive, dative, ablative, locative, and vocative—and more tenses and moods than we commonly think of. By contrast, English has worn down much more—in part because Latin was artificially reclassicized in the Renaissance. Indeed, English preserves an elaborate conjugation only in the verb "to be" (and, if anyone should ever use it, the verb "to wit").

Moreover, languages grow more abstract over time. Eskimos have a multiplicity of words for different kinds of snow, but no word for "snow." Tolkien turned Max Muller's dictum on its head, but both acknowledged, indeed proclaimed, the connection between language and mythology—and specifically between that "primitive" view of the world that sees many gods and spirits, in ash and oak and thorn, sunrise and sunset, morning and evening star, and that "primitive" state of language where there is yet no word for God any more than there is for "tree." Only with abstraction can there come such "advances" as philosophy, theology, or, indeed, this book. One cannot discuss "snow" with the Eskimo or "God" with the primitive: the ancient unities of their languages have not yet been broken apart.

Not only do languages change "on their own" (so to speak), but they borrow one from another. One can follow the movement of words from language to language and thus the movement of the things or ideas they represent from place to place. That approach to language has been one of the keynotes of philology for the last hundred years, and it can be found, suitably adapted, in the appendices to *The Lord of the Rings*. It is a kind of antiquarianism, perhaps, or a kind of genealogy of words (and things); the important thing to be noted here is that this too is a version of the past alive in the present.

Those who have read the appendices to *The Lord of the Rings* will recall Professor Tolkien's discussion of the problems of translation (in Appendix F):

> [The] whole of the linguistic setting has been translated as far as possible into terms of our own times.... Translation of this kind is, of course, usual because inevitable in any narrative dealing with the past. ... But I have gone beyond it. [My] procedure perhaps needs some defence. It seemed to me that to present all the names in their original forms would obscure an essential feature of the times as perceived by the Hobbits[:] ... the contrast between a widespread language, to them as ordinary and habitual as English is to us, and the living remains of far older and more reverend tongues. All names if merely transcribed would seem to modern readers equally remote: for instance, if the Elvish name *Imladris* and the Westron translation *Karningul* had been left unchanged....

And, similarly, the linguistic procedure by which the language of Rohan has been made to resemble ancient English speech "does not imply that the Rohirrim closely resembled the ancient English ... in culture or art, in weapons or modes of warfare, except in a general way due to their circumstances: a simpler and more primitive people living in contact with a higher and more venerable culture, and occupying lands that had once been part of its domain" (footnote, Appendix F). What is and is not to be translated further, in translations of *The Lord of the Rings*, is of course set out in Professor Tolkien's "Notes on the Nomenclature of *The Lord of the Rings*" in *A Tolkien Compass*.

I have sometimes thought that it would be an interesting experiment to ask a group of literary scholars, "What major modern work of fiction has as one of its heroes Banazir Galpsi?"—and wait to see how many of them (even the Tolkien scholars among them) would recognize Samwise Gamgee. (A similar question involving Kalimac Brandagamba— that is, Meriadoc Brandybuck—might not be quite so puzzling.) My point is not that the name of Banazir Galpsi is necessarily unfamiliar to Tolkien aficionados (it well may not be) but that the whole world of *The Lord of the Rings* as we perceive it is an English world, indeed a medieval English world, where Elves are Welsh and Dwarves are Norse, both being proper neighbors for this England. (It is true that the Elvish language has Finnish analogues as well, and Dwarvish sounds middle eastern, but the point holds nonetheless.) Professor Tolkien himself, as we have noted, referred to *The Lord of the Rings* as a work in which he had incorporated much of what he personally had learned from the study of things Welsh: this "Welshness" of the Elves, like the "Northernness" of the Dwarves and the "Old Englishness" of the Rohirrim, is not imaginary. The Northwest of the Old World in the Third Age is clearly the Northwest of the Old World today—the British Isles.

But much of this, according to the author, is a matter of translation. The paradox is that the translation is what attracts us. It is because we are reading about Sam Gamgee of the Shire, not Ban Galpsi of Siza, that we read on. It is not only the familiarity of the language and surroundings that we welcome, but their English familiarity. And yet by Tolkien's feigned history we are reading about what are, to us, prehistoric times (by C. S. Lewis's syncretistic reading, pre-glacial epochs). We may be reading about England, if by England we mean a geographic area, but it is not England in any other sense: the illusion that this is "really" England, as we know it now or in our history, is an illusion of translation, as I noted. But as I also noted, the illusion is more real than what underlies it, or is feigned to underlie it.

There is an explanation for this—indeed, two explanations. One is found in the passage I quoted from Sjera Tomas Saemundsson: "Languages are the chief distinguishing marks of peoples." The language, that is, defines the nature of its speakers. Thus the "Welshness" of the Elvish language means that the Elves themselves take on Welsh characteristics. The fact that the names of the Dwarves are taken from the *Elder Edda* provides a Northernness for the character of the Dwarves. When Gandalf is called by that name he is a Northern wizard, white-bearded and wearing a hat like that worn by Odin. When he is called Mithrandir he is different—more Elvish and thus more Welsh. And when he is called Olórin he is different again (though that is only once in *The Lord of the Rings*), being by that name an angelic being, part of quite a different kind of mythology. In short, the use of Old English, or Welsh, or Norse necessarily gives an Old English or Welsh or Norse character to the peoples involved.

This is, however, only one answer, or one part of the answer: it explains the appeal of the world-in-translation (so to speak), but it does not justify it. The other—or justifying—part of the answer has to do, I believe, with the fact that languages behave in the same ways, whatever the language, whatever the time—and with one other point. From the root languages, dialects develop, and these become separate languages (given sufficient time). The ancient unities of archaic languages break down, and the languages simplify (and at the same time become more abstract, or at least capable of greater abstraction). Inflections, tenses, numbers—all slough off. There is, in a sense, nothing new under the sun in even a new language. It is thus perfectly within keeping for a philologist, conscious of all this, to use one language in a given state of its development to represent another language at the same state, and to have the connotations of the one carry over quite properly into the other. This is what Tolkien has done, as he himself noted. If we assume that there resides some kind of *genius* in a land—a hardness in the Northern spirit, a kind of sanctity perhaps in the West—then we could expect, as languages rise and fall within that land, that the peoples who speak them will be not unlike each other. There will always—under whatever guise and in whatever time—be an England.

This may seem fanciful (though Tolkien's own statement quoted as an epigraph for this book suggests that it is not). What is not fanciful at all—what is quite certain—is that as the mythology of *The Silmarillion* underlies the story of *The Lord of the Rings*, so the languages of Tolkien's Middle Earth underlie that mythology. He himself has told us that the mythology was created for the sake of the languages. And here I believe we can find our way better if we take a detour into C. S. Lewis's grab-bag novel, *That Hideous Strength* (a novel which, admittedly, Tolkien did not much like). In that book, Lewis speaks of a language where the meaning is truly inherent in each syllable, as the sun is inherent in each waterdrop, "language herself as she first sprung at Maleldil's bidding out of the molten quicksilver of the star called Mercury on Earth but Viritrilbia in Deep Heaven"—a language of great words that sound like castles. This language, which Lewis calls Old Solar, is his version of Tolkien's eldest tongue, and I think it not inappropriate to use Lewis's lines as a key to Tolkien's belief, though here I speak under correction. (The reason Tolkien disliked *That Hideous Strength* was precisely Lewis's syncretism—his combination of Tolkien's mythology and that of Charles Williams.)

To see the connection between the sound of a language and the nature of its speakers, one need only contrast the Black Tongue of the inscription on the One Ring—"Ash nazg durbatuluk, ash nazg gimbatul, ash nazg thrakatuluk, agh burzum-ishi krimpatul"—with the language of the Elves— "A Elbereth Gilthoniel / silivren penna miriel /o menel aglor elenath. . . ." And it is not only sound that is important: syntax is also. To quote Tolkien's own commentary linking language and character (Appendix F):

> Orcs and Trolls spoke as they would, without love of words or things, and their language was actually more degraded and filthy than I have shown it. I do not suppose that any will wish for a closer rendering, though models are easy to find. Much the same sort of talk can still be heard among the orc-minded; dreary and repetitive with hatred and contempt, too long removed

from good to retain even verbal vigour, save in the ears of those to whom only the squalid sounds strong.

(Note here the phrase "without love of words or things"—a philologist's linking.)

Similarly, the language of the Ents (Onodrim) is "slow, sonorous, agglomerated, repetitive, indeed long-winded; formed of a multiplicity of vowel-shades and distinctions of tone and quantity which even the lore-masters of the Eldar had not attempted to represent in writing." It is like the Ents themselves—thus Pippin speaking of Treebeard's eyes (II, 83):

> "One felt as if there was an enormous well behind them, filled up with ages of memory and long, slow, steady thinking; but their surface was sparkling with the present: like sun shimmering on the outer leaves of a vast tree, or on the ripples of a very deep lake. I don't know, but it felt as if something that grew in the ground— asleep, you might say, or just feeling itself as something between root-tip and leaf-tip, between deep earth and sky—had suddenly waked up, and was considering you with the same slow care it had given to its own inside affairs for endless years."

There are other examples I could adduce. The hardness of the Dwarvish tongue is appropriate to a race working with stone and metal, even as its gutturals bespeak a people working underground. The shifts in the Elvish tongues—as in the names of the months—show a kind of "domesticizing" tendency at work (Narvinyé to Narwain, Nenimé to Ninui, Yavannié to Ivanneth, Narquelié to Narbeleth) that is at least parallel to—if it does not in fact denote—the "domesticizing" of those Elves that remained in Middle Earth in the First Age. The Sindarin language, like the Grey Elves, is more of the earth, earthy, than the Quenya and the High Elves. I use the word "domesticizing" advisedly (I hope) to suggest that both the Grey Elves and the Sindarin tongue over the years grew more at home in Middle Earth. Thus, distantly from adûn, the West, comes the Dun—of Dunadan, the Man of the West. But the Numenorean for "man" is atan and for "west" is adûn, less comfortable sounds. In the Shire, Baranduin becomes Bran-

dywine, and the Elvish name is thoroughly domesticized.
Follow where you will, in *The Lord of the Rings*, "languages
are the chief distinguishing marks of peoples. . . . Take away
the language and the people perishes, or becomes a different
people."

All of this is important for understanding Tolkien's version of Middle Earth. But languages not only reflect the nature of the peoples that use them (which we would expect
from Tolkien's scholarly work, even if we knew nothing whatever about *The Lord of the Rings*); they are also, in a sense,
the mirror of the action. Moreover, there are subsidiary ways
in which *The Lord of the Rings* reveals the contours of a
philologist's world. Here I am thinking not so much of Tolkien's verses (which are properly alliterative for the "Old English" Rohirrim, rhymed—perhaps over-rhymed—for the
rustic Hobbits) as of his word-play. By that I mean not only
puns (which are in fact few in number and concentrated
among the Hobbits) but the rhythmic prose in which Tom Bombadil speaks and the resounding anticlimax incorporated
in names such as Peregrin Took or Lobelia Sackville-Baggins.

It is in fact instructive to see how Tolkien played with
these names as he revised his work. When I was a member
of the University of Wisconsin Tolkien Society, our never-to-
be-finished project was a variorum edition of *The Lord of the
Rings* (the manuscript being at Marquette, in Milwaukee), the
first and only fruits of which were comparisons of the original Hobbit-names with those of the final version, a comparison showing Tolkien's attempts to achieve precisely this
effect. And if anyone doubts that this was habitual in Tolkien's own attitude to things, it would be in order to check
his verses on Charles Williams (printed in Humphrey Carpenter's *The Inklings*), ending with the reference to Great
Charles's Wain.

But let me return for the moment to language as a mirror of action. I will begin by calling to your attention the
hymn of the eagle that (III, 297) "bore tidings beyond hope
from the Lords of the West, crying 'Sing now, ye people of
the Tower of Anor/for the Realm of Sauron is ended for ever/
and the Dark Tower is thrown down.' " That hymn is clearly

and unmistakably modeled on the Hebrew psalms, though Tolkien otherwise virtually eschewed the use of any Hebrew models. It is fair, I think, to ask why this particular exception was made, though I will not answer that question just yet.

Some critics have objected to Tolkien's high-flown diction in those portions of the narrative that concern the Elves and the Men of the West, Eldar and Edain. The fact that *The Silmarillon* has not been as popular as *The Lord of the Rings* may testify to a general sense that elevated diction needs some relief or counterpoint, or it may testify to the vague sense of Biblical pastiche that seems to underlie the critical objections to Tolkien's use of this style at all. The word "Biblical" is, of course, misleading. We tend to think of Elizabethan (or even medieval) prose as Biblical because the King James Version— which was archaic in its own day, and thus very nearly medieval—is the only prose of that kind we read now.

But the style is equally that of Lord Berners or Sir Walter Ralegh—or Malory. Recall Sir Ector's lament for Lancelot: " 'And now I dare say, thou, Sir Lancelot, there thou liest, thou wert never matched of earthly knight's hand.' " Or recall King Arthur on the day of battle: " 'Now tide me death, tide me life,' said the king, '. . . at a better avail shall I never have him.' " Or (going on to Ralegh), recall the conclusion to his *Historie*: "Whom none could advise, thou hast persuaded, what none hath dared, thou hast done; thou hast taken together all the far-stretched pride, vanity, and ambition of man. . . ." Though Ralegh, like the King James Version, echoes the older style, it is Malory (and perhaps Berners) in whom we find Tolkien's model. Tolkien's persistent use of "and" to begin sentences, and especially to begin paragraphs, is strongly reminiscent of Malory. So, likewise, is the general "medievalism" of his tone—indeed, it is this "Malorian" quality to his prose that has, I believe, led to the widespread view that *The Lord of the Rings* is a medieval work. When Tolkien is telling of fair knights and ladies (whether of the Eldar or the Edain), he is using the diction of the most famous English chronicler of the fair knights and ladies of the Table Round.

Critics have also objected to the rusticity—still more to

the children's-story atmosphere—of the opening chapters
of *The Lord of the Rings*, characteristics that pretty much
justify the Inklings' calling it "Tolkien's new *Hobbit*." To be
sure, the style wavers a bit in *The Lord of the Rings*, while it
is consistently more childlike (or, pejoratively, childish) in
the earlier book. But rustic action, to a philologist, should be
told in rustic language, and a childlike narrative would be
appropriate for the doings of "the half-grown Hobbits, the
hole-dwellers"—those "Hungry as hunters, the Hobbit children / The laughing folk, the little people." When Frodo and
Sam sit on the right and left hand of the king, however, they
are *i Pheriannath*. Tolkien's use of different style for different
stages of the action may not be entirely successful—that is,
there may be technical flaws in his execution of the design
he has set for himself—but it is important to see that this is
what he is trying to do.

And this answers the question I posed a few paragraphs
ago. The eagle speaks in the mode of the psalmist because
that is the most exalted, most holy mode of speech that
Tolkien can use as (borrowing Eliot's term) an objective correlative for his action. (In the same fashion, when Aragorn
the King Elessar takes Frodo and Sam up and seats them
one on his right and one on his left, we catch an echo of
Christ and His apostles—presumably intentional.) Throughout *The Lord of the Rings*, the diction matches, or is intended
to match, the action. That there are problems with this approach is obvious, and two of them in particular deserve
attention here.

One, quite simply, is that we may not see the objective
correlative because we are not familiar with the object. We
may not read Malory. We may not all of us have read the
Psalms. We may not even have read the right children's stories. *The Lord of the Rings* was read aloud (first by Professor
Tolkien and then by his son Christopher) to a small group
who called themselves—and are still called—the Inklings.
They were not (*pace* Charles Moorman) a special group of
"Oxford Christians." But they were mostly men of a common
background, much of an age (except for Christopher), generally Tory in persuasion, and either Church of England or

Roman Catholic. We, on the other hand—we readers of *The Lord of the Rings* —are not a group with similar backgrounds. We are not all readers of Malory (though perhaps we should be). And we are certainly not all Tories. That Tolkien's voice comes through to us is part of his genius, but our cloud of unknowing does muffle it.

The second problem is that there is, as I have suggested, an air of pastiche to the whole proceeding—not to the use of language as a mirror of character but to the use of language as a mirror to action. C. S. Lewis once observed that Tolkien's world was like a version of *The Wind in the Willows* in which the battle of Toad Hall had suddenly become a serious *heimsökn* and Badger had begun to talk like Njal. Just so. And that transformation may not be to everyone's taste. More to the point here, it cannot be easy to carry off: I never, as a child, considered Kenneth Grahame's chapter on "The Piper at the Gates of Dawn" at all successful. As an adult, I admit I might revise my view, but in any case the shift is artistically dangerous. And if one shift is dangerous, what of many? Not long ago I picked up a paperback edition of some stories by the American regionalist and (if I may use the word) "pastichist," August Derleth. After reading the first few stories, I thought, Here is August Derleth being Montague Rhodes James. I turned to the last two stories, read them, and observed to myself, Here is August Derleth being H. P. Lovecraft. But where was he being August Derleth?

Now Tolkien is certainly being himself in the sub-creation of *The Lord of the Rings*: if the work is not absolutely sui generis, that is only because it has bred imitators. But there lurks at the back of the mind a not-entirely-organized thought that this high diction is "only" Tolkien being Sir Thomas Malory. We are used to authors whose styles are self-consistent. Hemingway's style is recognizable at fifty paces. Milton's style may go flat (as in the "untransmuted lump of futurity" that concludes *Paradise Lost*), but flat or rounded, it is clearly his. Wordsworth's style, though easy to parody, can with difficulty be confused with anyone else's. Charles Williams wrote a prose which is virtually inimitable (fortunately so, in the view of some critics). But what is Tolkien's style? The idea of *The Lord of the Rings*, the story, the peoples, the view of mythology, the whole sub-creation—these are recognizably his. The style seems to be another matter. Deliberately so.

At the risk of falling straight into the intentional fallacy, I would argue that the shifts in style are part of the philologist's world of *The Lord of the Rings* and that the approach has perfectly respectable antecedents. Not surprisingly, the one that comes first to mind is medieval, indeed quintessentially medieval. You will recall the Reeve's Tale in *The Canterbury Tales*, the northern "rim, ram, ruf, by lettre." You may also recall that the classic study of Chaucer as philologist (in the Reeve's Tale) is by Tolkien. But the Reeve's Tale is only one example of Chaucer's shifting style (compare *Sir Thopas*, the Knight's Tale, the Wife of Bath's Tale) and his use of language as a key to character. Of course, in *The Canterbury Tales* the action—that is, the tale told—itself reflects the character of the teller. Tolkien, on the other hand, orchestrates a vast polyphonic narrative, a feigned history, told mostly by one teller. He cannot shift narrators, and he cannot shift tales, because it is all one tale (though, to be sure, the past is filled in by Elrond and others). One could, I suppose, speak of *The Lord of the Rings* as an amalgam of Chaucer and Malory, but others beside Chaucer have fitted style to action (*Beowulf*, for example), and, on the other hand, Tolkien's whole complex endeavor is really something that has not been tried before.

I am no musician, but it has struck me that music provides an analogy for this use of style to represent action. That, in itself, says nothing of Tolkien's success. Beethoven used familiar themes to represent the English ("Rule Britannia") and the French ("Malbrouck"), and rifle-fire to represent rifle-fire in one of the most thoroughly atrocious pieces of music known to man. But if we think of words as Tolkien's notes, and the arrangement of words as a form of musical composition, we will at least be looking at *The Lord of the Rings* as a thing made, and its author as a maker, a poet in the Greek sense of the word. I said that what Tolkien essayed had not been done before, and now I seem to be saying that, in one way or another, it has been. All I am in fact doing is seeking analogies to explain this philologist's view of words and language and how it is given form and life in *The Lord of the Rings*. Things like this have been done before, yes, but not quite like this. (I would note, by the way, that this approach through music finds support in Humphrey Carpenter's view that young Ronald's lack of interest in the piano might be traced to the fact that "words took the place of music for him.")

It is now time to return to the other part of the philologist's view of language, the connection between words and things. In one sense, of course, the connection is that some words—nouns—are the names of things. Indeed, "noun" and "name" are both from *nomen*. But this, though true, is only the beginning of the story. The Orcs, it will be remembered, spoke without love of words or things, and we have already noted how this mode of speaking reveals the Orkish character. Tolkien's description of it does more: besides recalling this words-and-things approach to philology, it at least hints at a normative view of the linguistic process. It seems to be saying that those who love a thing will, and should, seek to enshrine it in beautiful words. Gimli, struck with the beauty of Galadriel, sought a single hair of her head, to be enshrined in imperishable crystal as an heirloom of his house: the skill of the Dwarves was in their hands, not in their tongues, or so it was said. But in the same wise, if we have any skill with words, we should seek to match beauty with beauty. Nouns must not only describe things, but suggest them, in a kind of onomatopoiesis. A noun is the name of a thing, as the old grammar books have it, but the question before us is one not so much of grammar as of gramarye.

For the plain fact and the rest of the story is that words, and especially names, are magic. It is fitting and proper that the gates of Moria should open to a magic word. It is fitting and proper that in the very depths of the earth, the deepest evil of all (deeper than Sauron, deeper even than the Balrogs) is nameless (II, 134) and that Gandalf, returned thence, will not speak of it. It is fitting and proper (and a related point) that the enemies of Mordor will not mention the name of

Mordor, and that a rebuke follows a lighthearted Hobbit reference to Frodo as the Lord of the Rings.

I am reminded of an old joke about Adam and Eve on naming day in Eden. Eve suggests to Adam that a particular beast be called a rhinoceros, and when asked why, responds, "It looks more like a rhinoceros than anything we've seen yet." The joke is, if funny, anti-Platonic: that is, it assumes there is no pre-existing idea of *rhinoceros* to which the beast in question can be compared. But if there is a "proper" name—a "real" name—for every beast, then to know that name is to know the beast, and, more important here, to speak that name, as our books of lore tell us, is to control the beast. Nor does this hold only for beasts. When Treebeard cautions the Hobbits about their hastily revealing their real names, what they call themselves; when it is recounted that the Dwarves reveal their true names to no one; when Gandalf, on his return, says that Legolas and Gimli and Aragorn "may still call me Gandalf"—we are at the edges of the realm where names are magic. If your enemy knows your name, he may command you. In the nineteenth century, when an African king died, his name passed out of the language, lest it be spoken thereafter and the speaker command the king's spirit. And the vowel-less Name of God, the Tetragrammaton, could be pronounced only by the High Priest in the Holy of Holies on the Day of Atonement. Clearly, we are not far from this naming magic.

Like other children of the eighteenth century, the science of philology reached its period of greatest achievement (and greatest excitement) around the end of the nineteenth. The New English Dictionary was and is a measure of that achievement, but there are other measures. There was a sudden interest in African and other exotic languages, marked by the publication of classic studies of tongues in the Rhodesian and Nigerian areas, ethnolinguistic research in Papua, studies of Amerindian speech, the rebirth (however artificial) of the Welsh and Irish languages. Certainly one of the things that gave impetus to philological study was the discovery of new languages in hitherto unexplored areas. It might be said that, just as the Edwardian adventure story had its roots in the great explorations of the nineteenth century, so in part did the philological impulse. A generation of scholars—of whom Tolkien was one of the last—was caught in a web of words that stretched from India (where, in effect, it began with the researches of Sir William Jones) all the way around the world to the South Pacific.

This web stretched, and stretches, both in time and space. It is a long tale, and not unlike the tale of the years of Middle Earth:

> "But that's a long tale, of course, and goes on past the happiness and into grief and beyond it—and the Silmaril went on and came to Eärendil. And why, sir, I never thought of that before! We've got—you've got some of the light of it in that star-glass that the Lady gave you! Why, to think of it, we're in the same tale still! It's going on. Don't the great tales never end?"
>
> "No, they never end as tales," said Frodo (II, 408).

I said in the last chapter that the difference between the brief (even slapdash) creation of such books as *King Solomon's Mines* or *The Lost World* and the long, slow growth of *The Lord of the Rings* was in part attributable to the influence of Tolkien's professional life. In part it is the difference between a scholar's sub-creation and that of a professional writer, by which I mean one making a living from his writing. But it is also the difference between a writer accustomed to following words and languages over the sweep of centuries and continents, and one not so accustomed. This is not to say that Haggard, in particular, does not from time to time feel the fascination of languages: it was, after all, the Shard of Amyntas in *She* that may have helped set Professor Tolkien on the road to his life's work. But only Tolkien wrote an Edwardian adventure story with the sweep of the philologist's world.

I had originally thought of approaching Tolkien's Middle Earth through its specifically medieval characteristics— writing of the "medievalist's world" of *The Lord of the Rings* — and certainly that would not be a difficult approach to take. But this approach through "medievalism" has been taken in the past, and the results have not been especially encouraging. Moreover, C. S. Lewis was a medievalist, but for all his close friendship with Tolkien, the world of his novels is not much like the world of Tolkien's, except where he is borrowing from Tolkien's world. When one contrasts the hit-or-miss eclecticism of the Narnia stories (especially *The Lion, the Witch, and the Wardrobe*) with Tolkien's careful use of linguistic objective correlatives, one can see just how much difference Tolkien's philology made. For Lewis, though a medievalist, and though a student of words (as in his *Studies on Words*), was not a philologist and did not think or write like one. Tolkien did.

Lewis writes in pictures. Indeed, most of his books begin with pictures, and his approach is essentially visual. Tolkien's is not. One can draw pictures from his words, but the pictures are one's own, not his. That is, of course, part of the use of language as a correlative for action, which is one of the four ways in which the world of *The Lord of the Rings* is a philologist's world.

Let me give some examples of this "non-pictorial" nature of *The Lord of the Rings*. A notable passage is Tolkien's description of Théoden riding forth to battle:

> With that he seized a great horn from Guthlaf his banner-bearer, and he blew such a blast upon it that it burst asunder. And straightway all the horns in the host were lifted up in music, and the blowing of the horns of Rohan in that hour was like a storm upon the plain and a thunder in the mountains (III, 137, 138).

A few lines later comes what is ostensibly visual description: "His golden shield was uncovered, and lo! it shone like an image of the Sun, and the grass flamed into green about the white feet of his steed. For morning came, morning and a wind from the sea. . . ." Here we have colors, but we create the picture; it is not created for us. Similarly, the description of Aragorn's coming in with the captured fleet is almost entirely auditory:

> Thus came Aragorn son of Arathorn, Elessar, Isildur's heir, out of the Paths of the Dead, borne upon a wind

from the Sea to the kingdom of Gondor; and the mirth of the Rohirrim was a torrent of laughter and a flashing of swords, and the joy and wonder of the City was a music of trumpets and a ringing of bells (III, 150).

And, a few paragraphs later, there is a passage that at first seems to be visual description, but is not really so: "Then the Sun went at last behind Mindolluin and filled all the sky with a great burning, so that the hills and the mountains were dyed as with blood; fire glowed in the River, and the grass of the Pelennor lay red in the nightfall." Here, once more, we have colors—or rather, one color—but it is the words and the connotations they bear out of which we construct the picture.

Not only do the auditory images precede the visual, but the visual images are of a particular and unusual kind. Tolkien is not always describing so much as "connoting." It is the approach of an author peculiarly conscious of words as words. It is also an approach that virtually precludes the description of anything outside the reader's experience (whether actual or, perhaps, Jungian), which means that Middle Earth in the Third Age cannot be much different from middle-earth in the second millennium A. D.

I have already suggested that a philologist would find it appropriate, given the universal nature of the laws of language, to use the language of one age and people to represent that of another age and people (assuming some similarity of nature), and that he might find it particularly appropriate if it is a people of the same part of middle-earth. One of the themes of Tolkien's work is the Englishness of England: that is at the root of *Farmer Giles of Ham*, with its story of Aegidius de Hammo and Chrysophylax Dives, *anglice* Farmer Giles and the Dragon. This theme of Englishness is combined with an un-English kind of art. It has been argued that the Englishness of English art resides in the view that the purpose of art is to preach, and the best preaching comes in accurately observing the detailed minutiae of daily life. In this sense, Chaucer is English, Malory is English (I recall that C. S. Lewis gave us some examples of this), C. S. Lewis is English, but Tolkien, like Rudyard Kipling, is not. Perhaps that has something to do with the fact that he, like Kipling, was enamored of "Englishry." Or perhaps it was because he studied the English language, partly from the outside, thus seeing it clearly, and with the same clear vision saw the beauty of Englishry.

To some extent, as I have suggested, C. S. Lewis can be used as a key to understanding Tolkien, and particularly Lewis's so-called space trilogy, since that was written during the time of Tolkien's maximum influence on Lewis. I would be confident in using *Out of the Silent Planet* or *Perelandra* in this way (though they are in fact not particularly useful for the purpose), but of *That Hideous Strength* I am not so sure. The Ransom of the first two books, who is, like Tolkien, a philologist, becomes in the third book a kind of Charles Williams, and the mythology grows Williams-ish as well (even though it contains references to Númenor). I cannot be sure that Lewis's views here are (if either) from Williams or from Tolkien—which is unfortunate, because one or two passages indicate a belief in an English genius, resident in the land. Such a belief would provide a philosophical basis for Tolkien's doctrine of translation. And it would help round off our explanation of the paradox whereby what is avowedly a translation of a feigned distant past into a recognizable England attracts us by its Englishry.

All this is not to say that *The Lord of the Rings* preaches a particular philological doctrine: Tolkien is no Levi-Strauss; he is not concerned with relating the structure of language to the structure of thought (or of being). No more is he a Dumézil exploring the structure of religion. And just as it is important to realize that philology does not explain Tolkien's achievement (however much it may explain his technique), so it is important to realize what Tolkien is not doing and is not trying to do. Because his Middle Earth is a philologist's world, there are several things it is not. Because he was a particular kind of philologist, there are several other things it is not.

Because words are used in the way they are, they cannot be used for pure description. I know from my own ex-

perience with the book that the connotations and linguistic
objective correlatives tend to outweigh the actual description. It was not until somewhere around the umpteenth re-
reading that I formed an accurate picture of the abode of the
Elves in Lothlórien. I am not sure how well I could set out
the seven circles of Minas Tirith. I could describe Bag End,
but what I would be describing, I think, is Badger's house in
The Wind in the Willows. In short, the philologist's world of
The Lord of the Rings is not a miniaturist's world.

It is not a structural anthropologist's world, either: Tolkien was emphatically not Levi-Strauss. I do not claim to
understand everything Levi-Strauss says, but it is clear that
to him the relationship of words (sentence and syntagm) is
more important than the words themselves. Words in language, like things in economic transactions, are counters in
a set of (chiefly triangular) relationships. The structure, not
the words, is the message. Now it is true that Tolkien was
not uninterested in language structure (the language of the
Ents, in particular, shows that), but it is equally true that the
anthropological approach to literature was largely anathema
to him. Indeed, when Lewis was asked to contribute an essay
to the festschrift for Tolkien's seventieth birthday, he responded with an attack on the anthropological approach,
ending with the words: "The forest is, after all, enchanted:
the mares have built nests in every tree." In short, *The Lord
of the Rings* is not a work whose world is to be approached
through structural anthropology—or, indeed, through any
form of structuralism.

In a way, this lack of interest in structure (even in this
peculiar sense) may seem curious in a world where relationships are of paramount importance, and still more curious
when that world is the sub-creation of a man particularly
interested in words and language. But there are relationships
and relationships—those that are irreducible or mathemat-
ical, and those that are personal or cultural. With the first of
these, *The Lord of the Rings* is not much concerned: it is the
relationship of master and man, of liege and liege-lord, of
companions in adversity ("we few, we happy few"), of king
and high-king, that are the stuff of Western culture and of

Tolkien's Middle Earth. We look not for new vision, new explanation of the way things are, but for ancient verities.

For philology, in Tolkien's practice, is historical—the past, as I have said, alive in the present. To be conscious of the past alive in the present, one must of course be conscious that the past is different from the present; otherwise there would be neither mystery nor excitement in its survival. The structuralist looks at what is constant, the historian at what changes or has changed. In his feigned history of *The Lord of the Rings* Tolkien is concerned with both historical minutiae and with the sweep of history, and because this is so, we respond to his world in a particular fashion. To a structuralist we might say, "Ah, yes, now I see the underlying patterns—now the way things work is made plain." But for Tolkien our response is "Yes, this is how Hobbits ought to speak, and how proud, brave, beautiful princes and kings must have spoken and acted in the great and romantic times of long ago." And our disbelief is suspended, and the long ago becomes part of our now.

You will recall, once again, Tolkien's reaction to the story of the juniper tree in Grimm, his perception of distance and a great abyss of time not measurable even by *twe tusend Johr*. We have come more or less full circle in our discussion of the philologist's world of *The Lord of the Rings*, back to the past alive in the present, and especially in language. I would suggest that it is not coincidental that the same brothers Grimm who collected the fairy tales were philologists—in fact, among the first philologists. I would suggest that Tolkien is their disciple in both respects. And I would suggest, finally, that those who see in him the teller of tales, though they are certainly right in what they see, are seeing something less than the whole truth. Tolkien's half-century of working life as a philologist caught him firmly in that web of words that is always and everywhere interwoven in his imaginative work; without that web *The Lord of the Rings* would be very different—indeed, it probably would not be at all.

CHAPTER III

THE TIMELESS MOMENT IN THE LORD OF THE RINGS: Christian Doctrine in a Pre-Christian Age

God is the Lord of angels,
and of men—and of elves.
Legend and History have met and fused.

J. R. R. Tolkien, "On Fairy-Stories"

Now God be thanked, Who has matched us with this hour,
And caught our youth, and wakened us from sleeping.

Rupert Brooke, "1914. I. Peace"

WHEN *The Silmarillion* was finally published, it made perfectly clear what had been seen in a glass darkly in *The Lord of the Rings*: Tolkien's Middle Earth is part of a Christian universe (though one in which Christ has not yet come). This contrasts rather oddly with the sometimes-heard (or -read) assertion that Tolkien's world is a world without concern for the gods. (I think I first came across that assertion in Mr. Carter's *Tolkien: A Look Behind The Lord of the Rings*, where Tolkien is compared unfavorably with Lord Dunsany in this respect.) But let us consider what a Christian universe before Christ's coming would have to be. After all, the 18th Baron Dunsany might wear his ancient religion lightly in those lighthearted tales whose greatest creation was that unfortunate king whom the gods decreed must not only cease to be but cease ever to have been. But John Ronald Reuel Tolkien—orphan, convert, Catholic schoolboy, emigrant—did not wear his religion lightly. As his biographer has stated (Carpenter, 103), he wanted his stories "to express his own moral view of the universe, and as a Christian he could not place this view in a cosmos without the God that he worshipped."

A Christian world in pre-Christian times must still be a world nurtured by the Christian God. Certainly there might be those who worshipped false gods. There might be fallen gods—true powers but demonic. And there might be, as in our own world, in pagan times, true gods or images of true gods worshipped falsely. It happens that, in *The Silmarillion*, we learn something about fallen powers, but we learn virtually nothing of them in *The Lord of the Rings*. Of the false or partly false worship of true gods, Tolkien had much to say in life (especially in the conversation that brought about C. S. Lewis's conversion), but little here.

Of course, in *The Lord of the Rings* there are angels

(*angeloi*, messengers), but they are far from being gods. We
know the angelic name of one of these beings—Olórin—but
he does not act like a Christian angel. In any case, the reason
for keeping the gods out of *The Lord of the Rings* may be the
inability to accommodate something like polytheism to a
universe of moral absolutes. Or the reason may be artistic:
each referent-language—Welsh for Elves, Norse for Dwarves—
has its own attached pantheon, and a multiplication of pan-
theons would be distracting. Whatever the immediate reasons, Tolkien has done what, as a Catholic, he should have
been expected to do: he has created a monotheistic universe.

It is true that, in *The Silmarillion*, there is a system (a
pantheon, if you will) set out along the lines Lewis imagined
in his Ransom stories—which are the lines Tolkien had set
out in that conversation fifty years ago. But in *The Lord of
the Rings* there is only fleeting reference to God ("the One"
in III, 392) and to the gods ("Valar"). The reasons for this are
essentially theological. Just as the ancient Athenians could
erect an altar to the Unknown God, but could not know Him
until St. Paul came to preach Him, so also the ancient peoples of Tolkien's Middle Earth could not know Him without
the preaching. And the preaching came with Christ.

Here I should take a slight detour. One of the unex-
amined questions about the moral world of *The Lord of the
Rings* is the presence of the wholly good (Aragorn, perhaps
Faramir, perhaps even Éomer) in what we assume to be a
fallen world. One senses a hierarchy of good, or a saving (and
unfallen) remnant, or both. Once again, I would turn to C. S.
Lewis for enlightenment. In *Perelandra*, the King asks Ransom if he does not remember that in the first generations
after the Fall, the people were long livers (to which Ransom
responds that most men take that for a story or a poetry).
The long lives of the first kings of Númenor (from Elros Tar-
Minyatur), though explained by what seems a different
machina ex Deo, are likewise reminiscences of a paradise
lately lost—but not, witness Aragorn, entirely lost. I am not,
of course, suggesting that Lewis influenced Tolkien—quite
the contrary. Be that as it may, the reason I bring this up is
to suggest the presence, in Tolkien's Middle Earth, of divine

powers and reminiscences of divinity—perhaps more than
reminiscences. The point deserves elaboration.

We are not dealing here with a Sprague de Camp sort
of world where the laws of magic replace the laws of science.
We are dealing with our own world, in a feigned past to be
sure, but one in which the same physical laws hold as hold
in our time—and the same spiritual and moral laws. "Good
and ill have not changed since yesteryear; nor are they one
thing among Elves and Dwarves and another among Men. It
is a man's part to discern them, as much in the Golden Wood
as in his own house" (II, 50).

Recall the First Epistle to the Corinthians (12:7-11), re-
counting the ninefold gifts of the Holy Spirit: the word of
wisdom, the word of knowledge, faith, gifts of healing, the
working of miracles, prophecy, discerning of spirits, divers
kinds of tongues (that is, speaking in tongues), and interpretation of tongues. It is the word "discern" that led me to the
passage in St. Paul, but the whole catalogue of gifts seems to
me highly relevant. For consider.

Wisdom and knowledge inhere in the Elves, the Wizards, and the Men of the West (perhaps also in the Dwarves,
though they seem, in a Christian cosmogony, to be dwellers
in Limbo, missing the Spirit). In Aragorn are the gifts of healing; in Gandalf the working of miracles; in Saruman and in
the Mirror of Galadriel the gift of prophecy; in all the Nine
Walkers except Boromir (and in Faramir, Éomer, Théoden)
faith, in some discernment; and in the whole creation the
gifts of tongues and the interpretation of tongues. The gifts
of the Spirit are present, and the Spirit thus abroad, in Tolkien's Middle Earth.

This is true despite the fact that no reference is made
to the Spirit, and only the one passing reference to God. And
the lack of such reference is exactly what we should expect.
If we understand—with those churches that accept the *fil-
ioque*—that the Holy Spirit proceeds from the Father and
the Son, "neither made nor created nor begotten but proceeding," then we must see that a theology consistent with
this doctrine cannot define the Spirit without knowing the
Son. By definition, in a pre-Christian age, Christ the Son can-

not be known, and neither can the Holy Spirit. At the same time, reference to the Father would be inaccurate without reference to the other Persons of the Trinity.

The claim has, of course, been made that Tolkien's world is non-Christian rather than pre-Christian—that he has taken the world of the Norse gods (or their English analogues) pretty much pure and undiluted. This claim sometimes takes the form of arguing that the world of *The Lord of the Rings* is essentially the world of Beowulf, overlooking the fact that the world of Beowulf is no longer pagan. But whatever form it takes, there is a certain power to the argument, and I would like to deal with it briefly.

The essential point is that Tolkien's Middle Earth has no Christian "feel" to it. The languages that he uses as objective correlatives do carry suggestions of the gods acknowledged by those who used the languages. Gandalf in his hat does recall Odin. So far the point is valid. But we are speaking of theology rather than religion, and the theology of *The Lord of the Rings* is uncompromisingly Christian and Catholic.

In what relation, then, do the Nine Walkers stand to God and to His servants? First, as we have noted, Gandalf is an angel, a messenger of the Valar. Second, Aragorn is one of the Men of the West, long-lived, of Elven descent, in a position analogous perhaps to that of the early Hebrew patriarchs, except that "being ... of the blood of the West unmingled" he is purely good, not mixed. Third, Legolas, being one of the Firstborn, is in—or capable of—a more direct communication with divinity than is possible for humankind (just how much more direct I do not know). Fourth, Gimli is apart, bound to Middle Earth, until "saved" by his love for the Lady Galadriel. And here we should pause to consider what is "middle" about Middle Earth.

Heaven and Hell, according to the medieval English lyric, are eating into merry middle-earth—Heaven from above, Hell from below. Middle-earth is not permanent in its present incarnation, neither in Tolkien's world nor in ours. We can expect, some day, a new heaven and a new earth, and in Tolkien's world, consider the conversation of Treebeard with Celeborn and Galadriel (III, 320-321):

> "It is long, long since we met by stock or by stone, *A vanimar, vanimalion nostari!* "he said. "It is sad that we should meet only thus at the ending. For the world is changing: I feel it in the water, I feel it in the earth, and I smell it in the air. I do not think we shall meet again."
>
> And Celeborn said: "I do not know, Eldest." But Galadriel said: "Not in Middle-earth, nor until the lands that lie under the wave are lifted up again. Then in the willow-meads of Tasarinan we may meet in the Spring. Farewell!"

Note here the word "nor." The meeting is not to take place in Middle Earth, *and* it is not to take place until Númenor is raised up. In a three-tiered universe, Númenor would be part of middle-earth. But apparently it is not part of Tolkien's.

In fact, Tolkien's Middle Earth is not three-tiered so much as three-directional. If the West is Heaven (or Paradise), then the East in some sense approaches Hell, even though the symmetry is incomplete, and Middle Earth is middle because betwixt West and East. This reading fits in with the land under the wave and Middle Earth as separate entities: by it, the Undying Lands remain forever beyond the circles of the world, reachable only by the Old Straight Track. By it, Númenor (or, rather, the Isle of Elenna) will be raised up, the world—Middle Earth included—will be changed, and the dead will be raised (III, 428). The distinction between Elenna and Middle Earth holds (III, 303, 390), and we may, provisionally, accept the view that Tolkien has shifted the "middleness" from a three-tiered to a three-directional universe.

At this point we are confronted with another theological question. If we put Tolkien's Uttermost West and all his West-Middle-East cosmogony into the same figurative category as the three-tiered universe, with the same kind of mythological truth, can we reconcile the truths behind (or within) the two? The myth—the cosmogony—is different, but the truth should be the same. To determine whether it is, we should continue the tale of the Nine Walkers.

Since the prevalence of the Hobbits is what chiefly distinguishes *The Lord of the Rings* from other tales of derring, and what (I believe) has determined its popularity, we should expect to find in their relationship to divinity something of importance to the theological world of *The Lord of the Rings*, and so, in a sense, we do. The thing of importance is that the Hobbits have, at the outset of the story, no connection with divinity beyond what has been handed on (languages, a few proverbs) from men and, ultimately, from the Men of the West. This would approximate a normal mortal condition, assuming Christian theology, in a pre-Christian age—with one qualification.

Aragorn, as we have seen, is unfallen, and Legolas also. Evil had entered into the world long before, in the person of Morgoth, but I can find no trace of original sin in any of the Nine Walkers, even Boromir. Temptation there is, to be sure, as with Boromir, and Pippin (with the *palantir*), and Frodo (at the Crack of Doom); and temptation can be yielded to, as with Gollum and, indeed, Frodo. There is jealousy between Elf and Dwarf, a certain stiffness of neck and loving of company in misery, but there is no universal predisposition to evil. In that sense we are in an age older than Eden, a pre-lapsarian state in which angelic beings are striving for mankind (and Hobbitkind). It thus becomes increasingly difficult to fit Tolkien's feigned history into our own (real, feigned, or mythic), unless of course we alter the story of Adam and Eve, or subsume *The Lord of the Rings* within that story.

The Hobbits seem thus to be without original sin as they are without God. By our own standards, their theological status is very odd—as odd as the idea of a yet unfallen world, upon which, indeed, that theological status is based. It is here that those who have objected to the absence of religion in *The Lord of the Rings* have put a finger on something of importance. For the progress of the Hobbits—Frodo, Sam, Merry, and Pippin—among the Nine Walkers can be seen as a progress toward spiritual awareness, toward the gift of knowledge if you will, indeed toward the gifts of the Holy Spirit generally. I might mention here Frodo's treatment of Saruman (wisdom) and understanding of what he is (discernment), as well as his foretelling Sam's children (prophecy); I might mention Sam's own gardening—in part with Galadriel's help—and especially the mallorn tree (miracles), as well as the general increase in faith and knowledge. Sam also has the gift of prophecy in his knowledge that "he had something to do before the end"—though the gift here is inchoate. And he and Frodo have something of a gift in languages—indeed, the knowledge of Elvish confers a kind of special status within the Hobbit world.

We can say, then, that although religion is absent in the Hobbits, surely the workings of the Spirit are there, more and more as time and the story go on. That the first state, in our own middle-earth, is rarer even than the second (which is certainly rare), does not alter the fact that the state is presumably characteristic not only of the Hobbits but of others in *The Lord of the Rings* as well.

It is not characteristic of Boromir, the last of our Walkers. Indeed, Boromir, of all the characters in the book, is most like us: a mixture of good and evil impulses. One could construct a critical system based on that fact, making Boromir the "hero" of *The Lord of the Rings*—a system not unlike that which, on similar grounds, makes Satan the "hero" of *Paradise Lost*—were it not that Boromir disappears from the action early in the story. It remains true, whatever our critical system, that the blood of the Numenoreans does not run true in Boromir: he is, in essence, a mere man.

Though this represents a problem in literary criticism (since the Hobbits are the "mere men" through whom the action of *The Lord of the Rings* is mediated and recorded), it is not a theological stumbling block. Boromir is one of the "nations" rather than one of the "people"—the gentile, the *goy*, the outsider. He falls, but recovers: yet though he recovers, he is clearly (from the very beginning) a lesser man than the others. To be sure, Númenoreans can fall: Denethor does, in whom the blood runs "nearly true," and back in history (as Appendix A tells us) Ar-Pharazôn the Golden broke the Ban of the Valar and set foot upon the Undying Lands. Yet there is a greatness in them beyond the greatness in Boromir—they would be greater in good or in evil (though, of course, Boromir repented).

What this portends, I believe, is not merely a hierarchical ordering of the sorts and conditions of men, not merely a celebration of a saving remnant, not even that *corruptio optimi pessima* ("the higher they are, the further they fall"), but a view that Christ and only Christ is the great leveler. In our Old Testament, though the chosen people can be aided by the *goyim* (Cyrus, King of Persia, being the obvious example), the chosen—the "people"—remain the chosen, and the gentiles—the "nations"—remain the gentiles. It is only in the New Testament, and especially in St. Paul, that the gentiles can be taken into the Kingdom. Similarly, in Tolkien's pre-Christian age, there is a distinction between the Men of the West and lesser men, and the Christ has not come to bridge the gap. Presumably salvation exists for these "lesser breeds" so long as they are not without the law, nor will it be a salvation different from that of greater men, except insofar as salvation is itself hierarchical (which, in Catholic doctrine, it is). However, it is just not the case that any one of the gifts of the Spirit resides in Boromir; thus it cannot quite be said that the Spirit is fully abroad, even among the Walkers.

One of the few attempts to deal with the theology of *The Lord of the Rings* is a brief essay by Deborah Webster Rogers, bearing the title "Everyclod and Everyhero" and ending with the observation that "individually we are hobbits; collectively we are Aragorn." I have elsewhere observed that Mrs. Rogers therein hit upon a precise temporal analogue to the doctrine that individually we are men, while collectively we are the body of Christ. On reconsideration, I am not so sure, since this would apparently make Aragorn a Christ figure, which he is not. Nor is he particularly a prefiguring of Christ. It is Gandalf who dies and comes back, not Aragorn, and it is the angels—the messengers—of God who take the place of Christ in pre-Christian ages.

I suspect it may be necessary here to examine the implications of the compound "pre-Christian." In one sense, of course, the word has a precise chronological meaning. There was a moment when Christ entered human history, in (owing to a slight Eusebian miscalculation) the year 4 B. C., and in this sense everything before 4 B. C. is pre-Christian. But the identity of Jesus the Christ with the Logos, the second Person of the pre-existing Trinity, the Divine Son whose Love for and from the Father is Itself the Holy Spirit—this renders the word "pre-Christian," in another sense, entirely meaningless. No Catholic (I should say, no Christian) can imagine our world existing before Christ existed, since He was the Word through Whom all things were made. There was a time before Jesus of Nazareth was born in Bethlehem. But there never was a time before the Second Person of the Trinity existed—only before He was known to exist.

Now the chessboard of time on which we live and move is merely the simulacrum of the eternity in which we have our being. The entry of the Christ into human history occurs on that chessboard—but also "before all worlds, God of God, Light of Light, Very God of Very God." It is only the knowledge of Christ (and therefore of the Holy Spirit) that does not exist in pre-Christian times. But Christ exists, and the Spirit also.

This lack of knowledge—which is dictated by Catholic theology—has led some observers to think *The Lord of the Rings* an irreligious book. It is not irreligious: it merely, and necessarily, portrays a world in which religion is not practiced as we practice it. Let me now return to a different and more debatable characterisitc of the world: the fact that it is (or may be) prelapsarian, that there is no inherent tendency toward evil.

Granted, this seems to be the case—but there is no inherent tendency toward good, either, at least in most places. True, the majority of Hobbits are only waiting for inspiration to attack the Boss's men. On the other hand, the men of Gondor distrust (most of them) the Lady in the Wood. There are Easterlings and Southrons deep and long in evil servitude (III, 280), but there are those who are not. In short, so far as outward appearances are concerned, it is a world much like ours (these Easterlings and Southrons might even worship pagan gods in the way discussed above). But the closer we look—at least the more inward the look we take—the less like ours it seems. It is a matter of "paiens ont tort et chrestiens ont droit": there is a kind of epic certainty about, and epic gulf between, good and evil. Only rarely, as in Boromir, do the two meet in the same character. Even Ghân-buri-Ghân is true to Aragorn. Even the King of the Dead is bound by his oath. If this is a fallen world, the fall is assuredly incomplete.

What then? Is this an unfallen world? With Morgoth in its history, nameless things gnawing its roots, Sauron mustering his legions, that too seems questionable. I am driven to conclude that this world is neither quite fallen nor quite unfallen, and this turns out to be in keeping with a three-directional universe. Middle-earth betwixt Heaven and Hell can be fallen, to all the round world's four corners. But when Middle Earth is middle betwixt West and East, the whole round world cannot be fallen (and, in any case, we have noted there is no Uttermost East, no Hell on earth). Moreover, we cannot draw a simple progression from West (Heaven) to East across the map of Tolkien's Middle Earth. Lothlórien is, after all, east of the Barrow Downs.

But perhaps this is not a fair example, since neither the Barrow Wights nor the Elves of Lothlórien are men, and it is with men that we are here concerned. (In another sense, of course, as Humphrey Carpenter suggests, Elves may be un-fallen Man, but this is not part of the theology of *The Lord of the Rings*.) Of the other peoples of Middle Earth, apart from those included in the Nine Walkers, only the Ents are not the creation of the Enemy (according to *The Lord of the Rings*): the Orcs and Trolls were bred by the Enemy in "mockery" of Elves and Ents. And the Ents, while they may become tree-ish, do not lapse into evil (though, curiously, trees may: witness Old Man Willow). At least within *The Lord of the Rings* it is only Men and Hobbits (and trees) who are mixed good and evil, and even for Men the West-to-East progression from Good to Evil is not complete, while for Hobbits (and trees) it does not hold at all. We must reject that supposition and conclude (despite some signs of this West-to-East progression) that the whole of Middle Earth is poised on the brink of the fall. It is angelic presences that have fallen, and some of mankind with them. It is as though Mankind, collectively (to borrow Mrs. Rogers' formulation) is Adam—the old Adam, though not in the colloquial sense: "Male and female created He them, and blessed them, and called their name Adam" (Genesis 5:2). And if mankind is Adam—which is what the Hebrew word signifies—then the One Ring, besides all the other things it may be, is the apple of the tree—though an apple of power, not of knowledge. Certainly temptation by the Ring is a common theme of the ring-bearer's journey.

It is not, to be sure, the only form of temptation. The *palantiri* tempt also (Pippin, Denethor, Saruman), insofar as they are engines of power. But the Ring is the great temptation, as it is the greatest power, and the subsidiary temptations should not blind us to the fact that the presence of this object of temptation in a world not yet fallen but poised on the brink gives a precise theological locus for the action: the precise moment in the timeless drama of temptation at which that drama has entered the time scheme of *The Lord of the Rings*. In the terms of our own drama, the apple is being presented to the Man and the Woman, the Serpent (that is, the fallen angel) is in the Garden, but no decision has been made. The Adam *may* remain unfallen.

I said before that in *The Lord of the Rings* trees may be sentient and moral—or immoral—beings. This fact may explain the inappropriateness of an apple (or any fruit) as the engine of temptation in Tolkien's world. I am not sure the question is of major importance as a matter of theology (it is obviously important as a matter of literary criticism that the object be appropriate)—except that it is important that the Ring is capable of providing multiple temptation. An apple, after all, if eaten by Adam and Eve, could not provide temptation for other men and women, if others existed. But the temptation in *The Lord of the Rings* is multiple: the Adam, as we observed, is collective.

A while back I noted the problem of reconciling mythic truths in trying to fit the theology of *The Lord of the Rings* in with ours. That statement may have been overly cryptic. Yet the more we draw the comparisons between Tolkien's world and ours—its temptation, the nature of its timeless moment, its prelapsarian (or its fallen) state—the more we see that Tolkien's theology is that of the Catholic church, as we would expect. But the shutter has been clicked—the exposure taken—at a different point in the process. Indeed, in the end, the Adam does not fall, at least not in the Third Age. Almost, but not quite.

This can be our world only if we can, in some way, make this part of prelapsarian, pre-Adamite history. Lewis, in *That Hideous Strength*, did just that. When Jane Studdock, in that book, asks where the jewels of St. Anne's come from, she is answered that they are treasures of Logres (which preserves the Numenorean tradition in Britain from beyond the moon or before the fall). But to do this is to beg a number of questions, one of which (at least) is important here. If we acknowledge this as our world (which Tolkien has indeed said it is), must the temptations of the Ring be part of the Adamite temptation?

The answer, I venture to suggest, is yes. Of course, *The Lord of the Rings* is not a theological tract, but it is the serious sub-creation of a Catholic and Christian author, presenting an alternative—or supplementary—mythology to the myth of Eden. And the congruence between the two is worth emphasizing.

Curiously, in view of the author's concern for language, it is only Gandalf among the Nine who tames animals with words (and then only Shadowfax). Names are indeed magic in the philologist's world of *The Lord of the Rings*, but for reasons having more to do with the paucity of animals than with any doctrine either of theology or of magic, there is little to parallel the myth of the naming-day. But the Hobbit ponies, and the trees of the Old Forest—and the Barrow Wight, for that matter—do answer to their names when they are called by Iarwain ben-Adar, oldest and fatherless, otherwise Tom Bombadil.

Doctrinally I find Tom to be Tolkien's least successful creation within the bounds of *The Lord of the Rings*. Standing alone, he would be a nature-spirit, an English woodland presence, both linguistically successful and a substantial artistic achievement. But he is not standing alone, and it is in this fact that the problem lies. He is not the *genius* (old sense) of the earth, since he is restricted to one part of it—specifically, the Tolkienian equivalent of Oxfordshire and Berkshire (Carpenter, p. 182). He is apparently a man, since he is clearly not an Elf or a Dwarf or an Ent or a Hobbit or one of the fallen races, but he is not one of the Men of the West. I suppose one could save the appearances by making him an angel, of a different order from the Istari, or by making him a god, but in both cases we would seem to be in conflict with Tolkien's mythology.

Perhaps we might make Tom a man, the untempted part of Tolkien's multiple Adam, and see in him one further way of treating the Ring. If the Ring is the Adam's temptation, Tom is that part of the Adam that, in primal innocence, does not feel the temptation. Though I find him an anomalous creation, I can make shift to account for him theologically— but only with the uneasy feeling that making shift is all I am doing.

Let me turn now to another theological question, on prayer and mediation. That *The Lord of the Rings* provides us with a world in which prayer is made only to interme- diaries—and particularly to Elbereth of the Elves—is clear. If God is the Unknown God, direct prayer to Him would, of course, be ruled out. But even the prayer to Elbereth is al- most entirely unlike prayer in our world, or at least as we generally conceive it to be here. For one thing, it works im- mediately and obviously. For another, it is more an invocation of a name than a petition. Even when the men of Gondor bow towards Númenor before meals, they are bowing, not praying.

This has to do, I think, with the nature of the mediation between God and Man. The world of *The Lord of the Rings* has not yet seen the coming of the one Mediator (and Ad- vocate) Jesus Christ, and with Him, his prayer. The power of God passes from Erú to the Valar to the Eldar to Men. (There is some irregularity in the process, as well as a problem with speaking of the Elves as unfallen, given Fëanor's actions as recounted in Appendix A, but these do not destroy the ar- gument.) The Elves, though they can be tempted, mediate the power of God, though not directly—and they do it not by virtue of office, as a priest, but by virture of Elfhood. Or do they? Galadriel, after all, is great among Elvenkind. We have in this world no priests, but have we a priesthood?

There are no formal sacraments (though there is certainly a sacramental quality to some of the meals, as Pippin's with Denethor), but are we in a sacramental world?

The outward and visible sign of an inward and spiritual grace—that, it will be recalled, is the definition of a sacrament in the catechism. It is also virtually an exact description of Tolkien's world and of Tolkien's art (in which even the use of language is sacramental). The triumphant language in which triumph is recounted is an outward and visible sign of what is happening within. The exterior beauty of the Elves embodies—perhaps it would be better to say "bodies forth"—an interior beauty. Orcs and Trolls and evil men are foul to look upon. When Saruman dies, his true character, masked by his arts in his life, is finally revealed. We are in fact engaged in a continuous process of minding true things by what their appearances be. And when appearances ("looking foul") do not truly represent an inward and spiritual grace ("being fair"), as with Aragorn as Strider, that fact is worthy not only of comment but of verse ("All that is gold does not glitter"). We are indeed in a sacramental world, to answer the second question posed in the last paragraph.

This, I believe, implies an answer to the first question, whether this world has a priesthood. In our own world, in our epoch, the priesthood (whether of Aaron or Melchizedek) is specifically ordained and differentiated from the nations not so ordained. One could argue that only in a fallen (that is, non-sacramental) world would there be this kind of priesthood or the need for it. In an unfallen world, any unfallen Man, or Elf, or Dwarf (perhaps), or Ent, or Hobbit could mediate divinity. Just as all acts could be sacramental, so all men (and Elves, at least) could have the power of Christ and of Peter.

It will be noted that I say "could"—the acts could be sacramental, the men and Elves could have the power. It is not certain that they would. It is not at all certain that the world, if unfallen, would remain so. Indeed, after completing *The Lord of the Rings* (if I have the chronology right), Tolkien went on to a planned sequel in which, about a hundred years into the Fourth Age, boredom set in, humankind being unable to stand prosperity for any considerable period of time. That is to say, temptation, having been conquered in the form of the Ring, started again in a new form.

Our own mythology makes the decision to eat the apple, the temptation and the succumbing to temptation almost instantaneous. Tolkien's mythology makes it a long haul, *per saecula saeculorum*. Because the Adam, once fallen, could not rise again unaided, we tend to think of the great temptation as a kind of "one-shot deal": once resisted, it would not come again. Lewis's *Perelandra* seems to be presenting this doctrine. But so far as I know, there is no reason to assume this would necessarily be the case. Our own experience in a fallen world—unending temptation—cannot be used as evidence here, nor can the fact that Christ made one oblation of Himself (once offered) be used to support the view that the Adam, once having surmounted temptation, would not have been tempted again. This is a matter not so much of received doctrine as of imagination: here, in other words, Tolkien's artistry is at work.

That his is a world mostly without gods and certainly without churches or temples—note the connection of the Hallows with kingship rather than priesthood—turns out to have reasons both profoundly theological and essentially Christian. That the sacred places thus depend on kingship might seem to introduce a political question, but to call it political would be to impose the categories of a fallen world on one unfallen. This, by the way, is a point from time to time overlooked in discussions of Tolkien's politics. He was, I believe, a Tory, and the Shire is a Tory Democrat's paradise. But kingship by divine right is theologically necessary in a prelapsarian universe, or at least in a Christian prelapsarian universe.

Let me turn to another matter. Theologians have for years distinguished the four cardinal virtues from the three theological virtues. Prudence, temperance, justice, and fortitude are supposed to be common to all systems (part of the *Tao*, in Lewis's terms), while faith, hope, and charity—or love (*caritas*, *agapé*)—are Christian. The same theologians have distinguished between mortal ("deadly") and venial sins, eventually agreeing upon seven of the former: lust, envy, pride, sloth, gluttony, avarice, and anger. It may be worthwhile here to examine Tolkien's universe according to these traditional heptarchies. If this is a pre-Christian world, but not prelapsarian, we should expect to find only the four cardinal virtues and all seven of the deadly sins. If it is a prelapsarian world, we should expect to find all seven virtures, and only one of the sins should be deadly: the sin against the Holy Spirit.

As we would expect, we find all seven virtures. Recall the constant emphasis on prudence for the Walkers and the Elven counsel of temperance to Gimli in the matter of the waybread. Recall the justice of the King to Beregond and the fortitude of the Hobbits. We have already noted the faith of the Nine (except Boromir) and we could as easily have noted their hope. And for the greatest of these seven, charity (agapé), we need only recall Frodo's giving his life for the Shire: " 'I tried to save the Shire, and it has been saved, but not for me. It must often be so, Sam, when things are in danger: some one has to give them up, lose them, so that others may keep them' " (III, 382). Beside this may be set Christ's pronouncement in the New Testament: "Greater love than this hath no man, that a man lay down his life for his friends."

Of the deadly sins, we find no lust, no envy except among Orcs, a tendency to avarice among Dwarves perhaps (but not in Gimli), little sloth, not much gluttony, some anger (Sam, against Gollum, with ill results), and a considerable amount of pride. It seems almost as though pride holds a special place among the seven, a kind of extra deadliness in Tolkien's world. And so it does.

Pride is (our theologians tell us) the sin against the Holy Spirit. Thus it is altogether fitting, within the framework of Catholic theology, that in a world informed by the Spirit, the one mortal sin should be the sin against the Spirit. All sins represent the exaltation of the self over others, but pride intrudes the self not merely in the relations of man (or woman) to man, but directly into the relations of man with God. It will be remembered that pride was Lucifer's sin and

(in wanting to be as gods) the Adam's. It is the sin that brought
about the fall, and thus it is the sin, above all others, to be
found in a tempted unfallen world.

Whichever theological road of inquiry we take thus
seems to lead us to the same point. The intersection of the
timeless moment with time is at the temptation of the Adam.
So long as the Adam is unfallen, this remains the point of
intersection, with no need for the redemption. Like us, Tolkien's characters must continually surmount temptation;
unlike us, they have no predisposition to succumb. (This
brings us back to the "fairy-tale" morality that Professor Walter Scheps has argued is inapplicable to our own world; it
is, however, perfectly—indeed, uniquely—applicable to the
world of *The Lord of the Rings*.)

As I said before, Tolkien has not written a theological
tract: his dislike of allegory in all its manifestations would
alone be enough to make that unlikely, even if there were
not a series of other reasons for not considering *The Lord of
the Rings* in that light. Chief among those other reasons is
the long, slow growth of Tolkien's creation from language to
myth to action. But it remains true, and important, that his
creation is theologically in accord with Catholic doctrine.
That fact explains not only the sometimes unsatisfactory results for psychological review of *The Lord of the Rings*, but
also the lack of "religion" in Tolkien's world. Theology, in
effect, pre-empts religion.

Why is this paradoxical? This age of charismatic Christianity, baptism in the Spirit, speaking in tongues, and healing seems not, after all, to be such an unlikely field for Pauline
theology to take root in. I agree. However, Tolkien's magnum
opus is the creation not of this age but of the time from 1914
to 1954—with, as I have suggested, roots before 1914. It certainly cannot be claimed that *The Lord of the Rings* produced
this revival: I strongly doubt it had anything to do with it. It
cannot be claimed that the two have the same efficient cause:
whatever produced the revival, it was not Edwardian literature, English philology, or the Birmingham Oratory. In short,
The Lord of the Rings was created in Freud's heyday, in a

kind of splendid isolation from the psychological world. Our institutions, our popular press, and our television shows mirror Freud. But we read *The Lord of the Rings*.

There is at least one loose end to tie up here, and that is the ultimate fate of the races of Middle Earth. To Men (and Hobbits) is given the gift, or doom, of men: to pass beyond the circles of the world, in death and resurrection. To Elves is given immortality, but not in Middle Earth. The Dwarves are clearly tied to Middle Earth, but *The Lord of the Rings* gives us no clues (that I have found) to their possible resurrection. The Ents, I suppose, go either with Elves or Men—certainly, as we noted, Treebeard and Galadriel will meet again. Presumably Orcs and Trolls will perish with their maker, everlastingly. Let me repeat that I am here restricting myself to *The Lord of the Rings*: Tolkien's theology is more fully developed in *The Silmarillion*, but I am looking only at the former.

"Without doubt they shall perish everlastingly." That line from the Athanasian Creed provides a Catholic definition of Hell, and one that fits into Tolkien's world. In our fallen days, the punishment of evil is timeless—Hell reaches back, so to speak, and infects even the former pleasures of the damned—just as the reward for good is timeless. But in an unfallen world—one whose timeless moment is before, not after, the succumbing to temptation—Evil, however personified, cannot have a permanent habitation within the circles of the world. As mankind triumphs everlastingly over temptation (however much by the skin of his teeth)—and this will, by definition, be happening so long as there is no fall—Evil must perish everlastingly. The world is not symmetrical because, in fact, Evil continually falls off the edge of the world. Though the gods—that is, the Valar—do not decree that it shall cease ever to have been, the decisions of Men, and Elves, and Hobbits, at least in the Third age, will decree that it shall cease to be.

And so it shall be—at least until it creeps in again. Morgoth was shut away, leaving Sauron and the Balrogs behind. Sauron was defeated, his realm—and indeed he himself—ended. But the seeds Morgoth planted grow and grow again, as his work is defeated and defeated again. There is no rest. But there is victory, and with that, within the circles of the world, we must be content. If that victory had continued, if our world was still at that timeless moment, our sacraments would not be confined to churches, nor our God to Sundays—and we would see *The Lord of the Rings* as a godly book, if not a "religious" one.

CHAPTER IV

TOLKIEN'S GENIUS:
Mind, Tongue, Tale — and Trees

A people without history
Is not redeemed from time, for history is a pattern
Of timeless moments. So, while the light fails
On a winter's afternoon, in a secluded chapel,
History is now and England.

T. S. Eliot, "Little Gidding"

God gives all men all earth to love
But since man's heart is small,
Ordains for each one spot shall prove
Beloved over all.

Rudyard Kipling, "Sussex"

"The incarnate mind, the tongue, and the tale are in our world coeval." ("On Fairy-Stories," p. 48)

W E have thus far considered the tale, and especially its Edwardian antecedents and Edwardian mode; the study of tongues and its influence on *The Lord of the Rings*; and the theology of Tolkien's approach to the Incarnate Mind. Can we, in these three, find Tolkien's particular genius and the reasons for the success of *The Lord of the Rings*? As the title of this chapter suggests, I believe there is one further reason, one further part of his genius, but that by and large these suffice. They may not be exactly coeval in Tolkien's development (though not far from it), but they are in the development of his creation. And whether we read the passage as describing how Tolkien himself went about his work, or (as I would prefer) we read it as discussing the universal process to which, *volens-nolens*, his own creation hewed, it still provides a key.

First, the Edwardian mode—the nature of the tale. The great exemplars of that mode—*She, King Solomon's Mines, The Lost World*—retain their popularity year in and year out, perhaps because of the adventures, but still more, I think, because of the mode. There is something very powerful in the image of the band of brothers abroad in the wide world, something very appealing in Tory England, something much attuned to our age in the idea of the past alive in the present, and something of great power in the commonplace narrator.

I once described the prevalence of Hobbits in *The Lord of the Rings* as an accidental goodness and took, as a result, a quantity of not-at-all-accidental ribbing from members of the University of Wisconsin Tolkien Society. It was of course accidental in at least one sense (as Carpenter has pointed out, pp. 199ff.) that the Hobbits, almost alone of Tolkien's creations for his children, strayed into his creation for himself. It was certainly a goodness, not only because Hobbits are the most ordinary of ordinary narrators, but chiefly for that reason. By a just instinct, Tolkien found his perfect plain men in the halflings.

Allan Quatermain, at least in Haggard's first books, is a plain, bluff man; a colonial, but very English in his character—English of those great days of Victoria's empire. John H. Watson, M.D., albeit (on some accounts) partly a colonial, is by consensus likewise a plain, bluff man and English of the English. Edward Dunn Malone is Irish of the Irish, but plain enough in that oddly assorted foursome in *The Lost World*. Even in the real-world antecedents of the Edwardian adventure story, as I noted in the first chapter, we find plain Englishry (of the "pukka sahib" sort)—albeit sometimes, as with Stanley, raised to the theatricality of "Dr. Livingstone, I presume." It is evident that this is part of the appeal of the genre, or Stanley—that most complex of plain men—would not have arranged this case of life imitating art. But why is the ordinariness of the narrator important to the success of the narration? Is it because we are ordinary? I think not.

For the plain fact is that no one thinks of himself or herself as ordinary. In one sense, of course, "you have never talked to a mere mortal," but that is not what I mean. I think we put ourselves not on Watson's level—though surely in real life we should be overjoyed to achieve his dignity, selflessness, bravery, and love—but between him and Holmes. We see ourselves not as E. D. Malone but between him and Challenger or Lord John Roxton. Yet at the same time we are reassured by the narrator's ordinariness. If this can happen to Dr. Watson, why then, it could happen to us. If Holly can sit before Ayesha in Kôr, we might also. The narrator's plainness serves the function not of making us identify with him, but of reassuring us that this strange adventure really happened. That—paradoxically, perhaps—is what the Hobbits do, and that is why this is an important part of the Edwardian mode. I do not know if earlier traveler's tales had this characteristic (was Sir John Mandeville a plain man?), but certainly it is highly important in the tales we are looking at here.

Of the past alive in the present, the more said, perhaps, the better. This is really (in the forests) the heart of Tolkien's

world in *The Lord of the Rings*, and it is the heart of the
Edwardian mode. It is, of course, a creation of the consciousness that the past differs from the present, and that the difference is not purely one of progress. The Middle Ages
recognized that change is not necessarily progress, but they
did not—as their art shows—realize that the past differed
from the present. Neither, for that matter, did the Renaissance. It is only with the coming of the Romantic view—the
appreciation of the Gothic, Strawberry Hill, Beckford's Folly,
Ann Radcliffe—and especially with Sir Walter Scott, that the
difference is appreciated. With Scott it takes root in popular
consciousness. Once there, it flowers rapidly. And it is still
flowering.

The flowering can be seen in the whole set of beliefs in
the occult that has given us *The Amityville Horror* and *The
Omen* (fulfillment of prophecy being a special case). It can
be seen in such staples of present-day fantasy as the Cthulhu
Mythos. It can be seen in the search for our roots as well as
in the anthropological approach to literature. All these appeal to the desire to have, or read about, the past alive or
coming alive *now*. The phenomenon has something to do, I
suppose, with the coming of the machines, with a perception
that the Industrial Revolution was a kind of fall from grace.
It is not, however, the same thing as that form of conserva-
tism that sees us standing upon the shoulders of giants (from
the past) or views the political process as a compact between
past and present. The difference between the two is precisely
that with the pygmies and giants, or with the compact, there
is no discontinuity from age to age; with the "past alive in
the present" there is.

This brings us, by a fairly direct path, to the idea of Tory
Democracy. In the first chapter I suggested that Tolkien's
Tory views, and those of the Edwardian Age, were drawing
us afield from our concerns. By that I meant particularly that
politics is neither the subject of stories in the Edwardian
mode (barring some of Saki's) nor even very important to
them. But then, Tory Democracy is not essentially a political
doctrine, as those who have tried to practice it have found
out. Winston Churchill may have been a Tory Democrat—

that is, by way of definition, he believed in an alliance between aristocracy and squirearchy on the one hand and the
people on the other. But he became Prime Minister only in
that darkest hour when England did come together in fact.
He is the exception that tests and defines (that is, "proves")
the rule. Only in 1940, not even in 1945, could Tory Democracy "work" politically. Otherwise, we must accept the doctrine that, in essence, Toryism in any form is that political
doctrine which avowedly prefers foxhunting to politics. As
a form of Romanticism, based on a love of the land and a
kind of longing for hierarchy, the relationship of master (say,
Frodo) and man (say, Sam Gamgee), it is related to Chesterton's Distributism and thus to the same impulse that leads
Americans back to the land on communes in Vermont. Nor
is the communal aspect accidental.

For finally—and we might equally well use the nexus
between Churchill and the Battle of Britain as our bridge—
we come to the idea of the band of brothers, the final qual-
ifying characteristic of the Edwardian mode. "Never have so
many owed so much to so few" could serve as an epigraph
for *The Lord of the Rings.* It could not serve for *King Solomon's
Mines* or *The Lost World*, because those are essentially private adventures—a fact which should give *The Lord of the
Rings* a substantial advantage over them in the public mind.
But all these works have the appeal of the happy few—which
is not (and this must be made clear) the same thing as the
appeal of the Inner Ring.

We are not talking about the fellow professionals, the
theme of so many of Kipling's stories from *Soldiers Three* on.
We are not talking about unofficial hierarchies (as in *War and
Peace*, to take Lewis's example) or about the strength of an
appeal that can make men together do very bad things before
they are individually very bad men. (This Lewis dealt with,
in particular, in *That Hideous Strength*.) We are talking about
the one sense in which *The Lord of the Rings* is certainly a
quest—but I would rather say a "task"—narrative: the sense
of great purpose that overshadows and ennobles the characters. Let me give a brief example of what I mean—not from
Tolkien's works.

Consider the following chapter titles: "There Are Heroisms All Around Us"; "It's Just The Very Biggest Thing In The World"; "The Most Wonderful Things Have Happened"; "Those Were The Real Conquests"; "Our Eyes Have Seen Great Wonders." Without further knowledge, to what would we assume these belong? Certainly not to most of our present-day novels, nor to any novel of character. Perhaps to something like a pageant, perhaps even to an imitator of Tolkien, or perhaps (but here we may be led by their appearance in this context) to an adventure story in the Edwardian mode. They are, in fact, the titles to chapters 1, 4, 10, 14, and 15 of *The Lost World*, and there is about them that sense of purpose I mentioned above. It is especially important that it is "Our" rather than "Mine" eyes that have seen great wonders—a notable contrast for our present age of anomie and alienation.

For that, in the end, may be what explains the power of this image of the band of brothers. As we are increasingly set apart from our fellow men, we fall either into individualism in Tocqueville's old bad sense (into Bishop Bossuet's "every man his own church"), or into the heresy of confusing the Inner Ring, fashioned perhaps from a shared skill but existing largely for its own sake, with the band of brothers that exists for some great purpose. ("For he who fights with me today/ Shall be my brother, be he ne'er so vile/ This day shall gentle his condition"—a pleasant irony, quoting Shakespeare to illuminate Tolkien.) In the United States today, policemen call themselves brothers, as do black men, but, for the most part, a sense of brotherhood is sadly lacking. This may be one reason for the widespread appeal of professional sports: fans otherwise sundered and separate are given the sense of belonging. (The theme song of the Pittsburgh Pirates is "We Are Family," as the country came to know during the 1979 baseball season.)

Now it is to this need for belonging that the very idea of a company of heroes speaks. For all that Frodo and Sam are master and man, there are Nine Walkers, not two, and that fact, I would argue, is highly—perhaps transcendently—important for the book's appeal. Like the appeal of the past in the present, the appeal of the company comes

from our rootlessness and alienation. I do not think it is
because we identify with one member of the company and
are comforted to find the others around us. Rather it is the
very idea of the company that gives us comfort—and, indeed, "comfort" ("strength-with") is a highly appropriate word.

It is therefore particularly important that we never follow the adventures of a single figure for any significant length
of time in *The Lord of the Rings*: even when we follow only
one of the Walkers, he is with new companions. When Gandalf goes alone into the depths with the Balrog, we do not
follow him. When Merry and Pippin are dressed as knights
of Gondor and the Mark, that is the sign they have found
new companions in their endeavor—not that they have left
the old. This is a polyphonic narrative of companies, not of
individuals: when Sam leaves Frodo it is a wrong choice in
more ways than one.

This much Tolkien shares with his Edwardian peers. It
is, as we have said, in the concern with language—in the
philologist's world—that he parts company with them. It
is here also that he parts company with much of the modern
world. Our writers "indicate" rather than "say"; policemen in
the Watergate case "responded" rather than "went" (or even
"proceeded") to the floor where the break-in occurred; offi-
cial Washington mushes through page upon page of regu-
lations or announcements in bureaucratese, whose lack of
style is matched only by its lack of clarity. I know of one
economist whose English seemed particularly dense and
who, when questioned, confided that he did not think in English but in computer symbols.

Do we miss this clarity, this style? We do. Even as we
speak the gibberish, we reject it, or are at least conscious of
its insufficiency. We revenge ourselves upon it by finding
beauty in the monosyllabic four-letter-word juvenility of street
speech. To be sure, that speech is capable of both strength
and accuracy, even poetry, but it rarely achieves it, achieving
instead the dreary repetitions of the Orc-minded. In short,
language currently seems to approximate the exact contrary
to the "speaking in tongues" of charismatic or pentecostal
Christianity. Rather than seeming to be meaningless, but really

having meaning, bureaucratese and gutter-speech alike appear to have meaning but do not. No wonder we feel the lack.

Now whatever can be said of Tolkien's achievement, there is no question whatever that he uses words accurately and with unusual forethought, even on occasion with that pedantic accuracy which is in effect a play on words (the "Tale of Years"). We may sometimes sense a "Biblical" pastiche, but the same impulse that has led men to impute Biblical authority only to the "sacred English original"—to quote the story told by Miss Sayers—also leads us to welcome the familiar elevated diction and (possibly) rhythms. Whereas, a generation ago, the Bible and Shakespeare were only two constellations in a star-spangled sky of familiar great literature, these days the lights are going out all over the Western world, and even the Bible is more common in hotel rooms than in living rooms. But the memory lingers. A faint breath reaches even the late generations.

The naming and the language, then, are also part of Tolkien's appeal, though that is by way of being an accident. He may have set out to write an Edwardian adventure story (or a secondary epic following nature) when Allen & Unwin asked for a sequel to *The Hobbit*. He did not set out to appeal to our sense of the lost beauty and nobility of language; that appeal happened because of what he was. And he was as surprised by it as any. This is what we would expect of *genius* in the old sense; or, to put it another way, it is part of a sense of humor in the Muse. Be that as it may, one need only compare Tolkien's names with those of, say, E. R. Eddison (Lord Gro, Koshtra Pivrarcha) to see a naturalness in one, an appeal to an unremembered past perhaps, and in the other no more than a set of suggestive syllables. Yet Eddison was praised for his naming.

And the Incarnate Mind—the Mind of the Maker? We have drawn from *The Lord of the Rings* a familiar theology. We have seen a universe poised at a timeless moment different from ours, but in the same process of temptation. We have glimpsed the Holy Spirit abroad in Tolkien's world, and the gifts of the Spirit. This is indeed part of our universe, and we can say that the Poet who uttered it through J. R. R. Tolkien is the Same through whose Word our world was made. Quite so. But in what way does this aid Tolkien's appeal?

There can be several ways of answering this question. We could say—Tolkien would himself say—that we recognize the Original Maker in the act of sub-creation. In the essay quoted at the outset of this chapter he has, in fact, said something very much like that. This we may call the theological answer. Or we could say that the timeless drama of temptation, the sense of great powers moving, the mixed familiarity and strangeness of what happens within us happening within the nations and peoples of Middle Earth, are what speaks to us—especially if we are reassured somehow by the presence of unfallen beings in the drama. This I might call a philosophical answer, and I suspect Tolkien would agree with it also. Or we might say that theological consistency imposes a particular character on any work of literature. That argument has been advanced by Miss Sayers in the essay quoted before; it may be called the literary answer, and it deserves elaboration here.

She made that point in the introduction to her series of radio plays on the life of Christ: "Except a man believe faithfully he cannot—at least his artistic soul cannot—be saved." Theological consistency, she was claiming (in defense of her own artistic endeavor), imposes a unity equal to, if not the same as, Aristotelian unity. Certainly the polyphonic narrative of *The Lord of the Rings* has unity neither of time, place, nor action: it is, after all, polyphonic. Nor—in comparison with *The Silmarillion*, for example—has it unity of language. Yet we perceive it as one work (at least most of us do), despite the publisher's expedient of making it a three-decker, despite the mutilation in the animated film, the slings and arrows of outrageous fortune-hunting. Miss Sayers would have answered, as I say, that this unity we feel is theological. But what does that mean and how does it work? After all, most of us are close to being theological morons, either because we do not believe at all or because, having found God, we see no need for mapping His being. Theological consistency is not, on the face of it, something we value.

But we value *The Lord of the Rings*, and not least because we feel its unity. It is not merely that Men, Elves, Wizards, Dwarves, Hobbits, Ents, Orcs, and Trolls all act in character, though that in itself is part of this theological unity. After all, acting in character is part of many works of literary art. It is not merely that there is a sense of proportion, of part to part and of the parts to the whole. That also is true, and something of what Miss Sayers was talking about, but it is nothing like a full explanation. It is rather, I would argue, that this theological unity is itself mythopoetic. That is, the proper literary embodiment of theology is myth, or the creation of myth—mythopoeisis. Allegorical presentations, if they do not achieve myth, descend to mere personification, bearing to literature the same relation that mnemonic verses bear to poetry. That much has been noted. But it should be emphasized that myth is the natural result of theological concern, and especially that the more complete and consistent the theology, the more perfect the myth. Let me make it clear that by *mythopoeisis* I do not mean, generally, fantasy in Tolkien's sense, but precisely the making of myth.

Perhaps the connection between mythmaking and theology has been most widely acknowledged in criticism of Melville's *Moby Dick*. Not only is the myth of the great sea creature a powerful one, particularly in the United States— witness the recent success of the movie *Jaws*—but critics have almost universally asked questions exhibiting the theological implications of Ahab's search. Is the whale evil? Why is it white? Is Ahab a personification of some particular characteristic—vengeance, perhaps (but " 'Vengeance is Mine,' saith the Lord")? Good questions, these, and nonetheless for having been asked so often.

What has not been so often asked, and what I would like to discuss here, with *The Lord of the Rings* as my major example, is why myth and theology go together. In part, of course, the answer has to do with a certain sweep—a certain breadth—implicit in both. But it has much more to do with the almost axiomatic fact that both myth and theology deal with gods. We may, to be sure, call them archetypes: we may

Platonize them or Euhemerize them. The fact remains that the creatures of the myth simply *are*, without explanation, without character development. Asking why they are, and particularly asking why they are the way they are, brings us immediately into theology, rather than into literary criticism.

Suppose we ask why Gimli was not tempted by the Ring, whereas Galadriel (for example) was. The answer, I suggest, lies in the very fact that Dwarves generically might be expected to be tempted by the Ring *as a ring*, as a golden object, and this lower-level temptation would be theologically irrelevant—as though Adam had been tempted to eat the apple because he was hungry. Or suppose we ask why Galadriel *was* tempted? Tolkien has given us the answer to that question in *The Silmarillion*, and Christopher Tolkien has added to it in *Unfinished Tales*: the answer itself is not important, but the fact that the answer is theological is important—indeed, crucial.

As a Christian, I would of course argue that the truth of Christian theology leads to mythmaking more satisfactory than that based on any other theology—in other words, that the Mind of the Maker is incarnate here. But to do so would in our present discussion be a prime example of question-begging. And in any case, mythmaking of any kind seems to appeal to our present age. Those who in the past few years observed books of "Jaws" jokes, stuffed sharks, and "Jaws" t-shirts and games can testify to that. Nor is it only our age: Fenimore Cooper's tales owed much of their popularity, I think, to their mythic quality.

Yet the theology implicit in *Jaws* is Pelagian if not Paleyite, though in a particular modern form of Pelagianism. (The shark is killed not by the Ahab figure or even by the academic expert on sharks, but by the apparently weak-kneed policeman who hates water.) The theology of Leatherstocking is Christian, though doubtless infected by those various heresies against which the first Timothy Dwight inveighed in his (and Cooper's) days at Yale: Natty Bumppo speaks not to the self-perfectibility of man but to his fall from natural grace. The fall from grace is, of course, the theological underpinning to the myth of the noble savage.

I would argue that it is the theology that captures the audience: we need to be told that our relation is to the scheme of things, to God or gods or the powers that be. But theology is not what the audience thinks is capturing it. What the audience perceives as its captor is the central mythic figure—the shark, Natty Bumppo, the Hobbit—and its element, its proper surroundings. For the shark, like Moby Dick (and here perhaps Jungian psychology could be used to illustrate our point), comes out of the depths of the sea, stirring (it may be) our racial memory. And Leatherstocking strides through the depths of the forest; the key word here may likewise be *depths*. Tolkien himself has recounted his own reading of those tales: "Red Indians were better: there were bows and arrows . . . and strange languages, and glimpses of an archaic mode of life, and, above all, forests in such stories" ("On Fairy-Stories," 63). And what of Tolkien's own creation? The Hobbits would doubtless say, if they said anything on the subject, that they were in their element at home in the Shire, and in one sense they would be right. But I know few readers to whom the chief appeal of *The Lord of the Rings* lies in the opening chapters, or even in the Scouring of the Shire. The chief element in which the book functions—Hobbits and all—is the forested earth.

Elementary, you say—though perhaps not so many have seen it as should have—partly because the Hobbits have in a way strayed from another book, another set of stories, into the world of the Ents, the forests at the heart of *The Lord of the Rings*. In *The Silmarillion*, if I may be permitted the digression, Tolkien feigns that trees are the leaders, so to speak, of the vegetable kingdom, a point which could be deduced from *The Lord of the Rings* but which is not explicit there. We have already noted that trees can turn to evil, that they are sentient and capable of being tempted (on which, also, *The Silmarillion* provides further detail). They are, in short, characters in the story—but they and their forests are much more.

There were olden days when a squirrel could go from tree to tree across Middle Earth; Mirkwood and the Old Forest are relics of those days. The Galadrim are tree-dwellers.

The White Tree is the sign of the King's return. Even the Party
Field in the Shire centers on a tree—first the Party Tree, then
the mallorn. Mellŷrn also play a part in the elegy for Arwen
and Aragorn ("There at last, when the mallorn-leaves were
falling, but spring had not yet come..."). We need only look
at *The Lord of the Rings* for the briefest of times to catch a
vision of ancient forests, of trees like men walking, of leaves
and sunlight, and of deep shadows.

But why is this world of forests so appealing? To that
there are at least three possible answers. First, it may be that
forests are part of the Jungian memory. Second, it may be
(as has certainly been suggested) that Tolkien's love of countryside and distrust of progress is in tune with our Aquarian
age of ecology. Third, it may be that the first answer is unnecessarily profound, and the second unnecessarily restric-
tive and specific; perhaps we should say only that men love
trees, and the "citification" of the Western world has made
them more precious than ever. In other words, Tolkien's appeal to us may be Fenimore Cooper's appeal to Tolkien.

It may be the trees we love, or the tale, or the tongues,
or the Incarnate Mind, or it may be all of these (as I think it
is). But why is it Tolkien? Why did John Ronald Reuel Tolkien,
of all people, create *The Lord of the Rings*? To some degree,
we have answered that question, by looking at the years and
reading of his youth, at his life's work, and at his life's belief.
But other Christian philologists grew to manhood in Tolkien's generation. They may have read his creation with
enjoyment, but they did not create it. They did not characteristically respond to a work of medieval literature by
writing another in the same mode. They did not create Hobbits for their children. They may have written light verse or
war poetry or books for children. If they were exactly of his
generation they would surely have written war poetry, or
poetry after the mode of Rupert Brooke. But that poetry did
not become part of a Silmarillion or a song of Middle Earth.
What was the particular genius of this member of the King
Edward's School Rugger XI, of the Tea Club, Barrovian Society,
of the Lancashire Fusiliers (Lieutenant), of the OED and Leeds
and the University of Oxford (D. Litt.), and the Order of the
British Empire (Commander)?

One could answer, I suppose, that the *genius* attaches itself to the man as a kind of tutelary spirit. One could as well answer that the Muse strikes as she wills, not as we will. It is true. It has the form of an answer. But was it merely the Muse's jest to select Tolkien, a Hobbit himself, to create *The Lord of the Rings*? It was no jest. For the final thing we must note about *The Lord of the Rings* is that its success depends on the interplay of Hobbits and ancient world. Like Hobbits, we cannot live very long on the heights. We need rusticity amid our elevated diction, plain gardens amid our forests, inns amid our pleasures and palaces. And the answering of that need is what, in the end, defines Tolkien's genius. With all the other things he was—Edwardian, Tory, philologist, Roman Catholic—he was, finally, and forever is the image of Frodo Baggins. It was noted before that Hobbits strayed from stories he told his children into this greater story: it was noted that Hobbits are an accidental goodness. Just so, but the accident—the straying—was contrived by the Muse. Not in jest. In earnest.

Now the Hobbits, though self-portraits, are self-portraits at the age of forty (or more). The Elves, and most of the rest of *The Lord of the Rings*, have origins in Tolkien's youth. (The Ents, given that Treebeard's "Hoom, Hoom" is modeled on C. S. Lewis, are later.) The shift from the high style, the elevated diction, to quiet rusticity, is partly a shift in viewpoint from youth to middle age, though Hobbits, like Tolkien himself, seem in many ways perennially youthful. This perennial youthfulness notwithstanding, and the frequent comparisons to children as well, the Hobbits are recognizably the creation of an older man. Had I wished to trespass further on Tolkien's private life, I could have discussed his four children, and his relationship with them; I have not, but the Hobbits are, in effect, part of Tolkien as father—more than as Edwardian, or philologist, or Catholic.

But, it will be objected, the comparisons to children are valid: the Hobbits are childlike (or childish). Yes, but they are not a child's or even a young man's creation. And in this fact lies, I believe, a part of the appeal of *The Lord of the Rings*. If the forests and Elves, the knights and ladies, and the "paiens ont tort" call to morality are in tune with a youthful romanticism (of a medieval sort), the Hobbits are a kind of reassurance that this youthful romanticism, this version of middle-earth, will continue to have meaning into our own middle age. Rather than the slow decline of youthful hopes, the wearing away of high ideals, the growing success of the world (along, perhaps, with the flesh and the devil), the cynicism and worldly wisdom of a creature accustomed to this fallen existence, there is implicit in *The Lord of the Rings* a promise. We are promised that within as well as beyond our workaday being there is high adventure, great peril, and the possibility of success in something other than worldly goods. We are assured that the Elven world we longed for is there— somewhere—however much we, like Tolkien, are Hobbits.

We seem to have come a long way from the Edwardian adventure story with which we started back in Chapter I. That pre-existing mode, apparently a slight and merely popular thing, is carrying a whole world for ballast and the Holy Ghost for mast—what have Rider Haggard and Conan Doyle to do with this? Even if we call it not an Edwardian adventure story but a particular kind of secondary epic following nature, its immediate literary forebear is still Haggard, and it is still in the Edwardian mode as we have defined it. At the beginning of this chapter I considered the peculiar appeal of this mode, and particularly that part of it I defined as "the past alive in the present." Could it be that this "adventure story in the Edwardian mode"—perhaps as a result of this characteristic—is in fact a far greater thing than we have believed it to be? I mentioned that its characters are types who sometimes (as with Holmes) rise to the dignity of archetypes. Could this be an indication that the Edwardian mode, whether we call it adventure story or epic, is mythopoetic?

Haggard was praised by C. S. Lewis as a mythmaker. Sherlock Holmes will live always in our minds at 221B Baker Street, with Mrs. Hudson below and Victoria on her throne. Is this perhaps part of the secret? Is *The Lord of the Rings* the apotheosis of something that was close to divinity before Tolkien began writing? Even Jeeves is a myth. Even Bertie Wooster. Have we mistaken the quality of the genre? Are we in a way rendering to Tolkien what is not peculiarly his?

For every action, the physicists tell us, there is an equal and opposite reaction. For the Industrial Revolution and the myth of progress that spawned or was spawned by it, there is a counterrevolution and a myth of anti-progress. For the story of man's perfectibility, the magic that makes dross into gold and men into gods, there is the story of man's fall, the black magic that has made dross out of gold and men into devils. But suppose, just suppose, a world in which Eden, though it must be striven for to be maintained, has never been lost. Suppose we have a myth of anti-progress recognizing that change may be ill, but not that it is inevitable. Suppose the contending forces are not the machines on the one hand and King Ludd on the other: suppose they are the machines and the countryside, Eden not at the confluence of the four rivers, nor whose gate is guarded by the angel with a flaming sword, but Eden in an English shire. Suppose it is not the new Jerusalem but, miraculously, something older than the old that is builded in England's green and pleasant land.

Am I trying to weave a spell? Perhaps I am. After all, weaving a spell is precisely what Tolkien has done, and it is not accidental that *spell* is the word both for "incantation" and for "story." Tolkien, by his imagined past, is liberating us from our present, and still more from a future we perceive and fear. We are not, of course, the Englishmen for whom he set out to provide a mythology. We are not the Inklings. Yet we hear what he is saying, for all that we may be overhearing it, and we respond with a quickening of spirit. Frodo lives, and we with him. England lives, and with it, us. But is England's green and pleasant land so powerful a myth within itself that it refreshes us?

The question that concludes this last paragraph, and the one about rendering to Tolkien what is not his alone, may be the same question in the end. The Edwardian mode is peculiarly English, indeed the Edwardian Age was peculiarly English, even when transferred (in the person of P. G. Wodehouse) to the environs of New York City. Why does this vision of England appeal? There will always be an England, but is that any reason it should be firmly engrafted in American hearts—not to mention the hearts of those Dutchmen, Swedes, Japanese, Romanians, and all who have read *The Lord of the Rings* in translation? The intersection of the timeless moment is England (for all that it is a country of the mind) and always (for all that it never happened). But why is this important?

"God gave all men a land to love"—thus Kipling in praise of Sussex by the sea. But Kipling was born and raised in India, and came to England from his exile. So also Tolkien came—but much younger—from his birthplace in South Africa. The contrast between the arid land around Bloemfontein and the green of England was one of his first memories. He was—to repeat a point I made earlier—in England, loving England, but not of it. Since most of his enthusiastic readers are not of it either, that may be involved in his appeal to us. The question is whether another land could serve the purpose. Could the intersection of the timeless moment be France or Germany? Or must it be England?

Lewis, who was that most English of the non-English, an Ulsterman, would say yes, there is a particular spirit of England, different from the particular spirit of France or Germany. Even if that is true, why would this spirit of England be important to those who neither have seen the land nor descend from those who have lived in it? Tolkien's ancestry was English, as was Kipling's. Ours may not be.

But *languages* are the chief distinguishing marks of peoples. That is not merely something Sjera Tomas Saemundsson said, or Tolkien repeated. It is not merely a key to Tolkien's critical doctrines or day-to-day belief. It is true, and *The Lord of the Rings* is evidence of its truth. I cannot speak for those who read it in translation, and I suspect that translators into non-Germanic languages, at least, will have substantial trouble with their task. But we who read it in English are, as English-speakers, the inheritors of Tolkien's English mythology, heirs through that grace of his kingdom. By the fact of our language, whatever our ancestry, we are native to that northwest corner of Europe that is the scene of *The Lord of the Rings*. The timeless has intersected our English-speaking lives at an English moment: because Saemundsson's words are true, that moment belongs to us. *Si momentum requiris, circumspice.*

And that, but for some tying up of loose ends, concludes what I have to say. The principal loose end has to do with the matter of temptation: is it somehow illegitimate for us to be invited to observe and even participate in the long process of temptation in an unfallen world? Does this not cheat us by making us think things are easier than they really are? Granted that *The Lord of the Rings* is theologically accurate, is it not psychologically "escapist" in this way at least? Fair questions, these—but it is the purpose of Eucatastrophic stories to give hope, and the same theology that girds the world of *The Lord of the Rings* promises us that baptism overcomes original sin. In any case, Tolkien is not calling on us to take action, and his book is not a tract.

For we must be careful not to impute to a work of literary sub-creation the attributes of a Bible. Even if we find ourselves thinking in Tolkienian terms, using his characters and events to interpret our own lives, it is we who are doing this, not Tolkien, nor is he asking us to do it. During his life he accepted, even enjoyed, the efforts of his readers to apply to his sub-creation the same kind of scholarship he applied. He also strongly opposed those kinds of "scholarship" that looked at psychological journeys or involved any form of the personal heresy. He was a maker, not a psychologist, not even a priest.

This brings up a second loose end. I have from time to time, in what has gone before, explicitly rejected the use of *The Silmarillion* as a key to *The Lord of the Rings*. But Tolkien the maker made not only the one work, great though that is: he left many works, though this greatest among them. Why not look at them all? Why restrict oneself to this one work, when other parts might provide illumination (especially for Chapter III)?

To this there are two answers. First, I am specifically looking at *The Lord of the Rings*, partly because the continued success of most of the rest of Tolkien's oeuvre is derivative, partly because twenty-five years is long enough to wait

for someone to spend a hundred pages or so seeing what it
is that has become so popular. Second, so far as *The Silmarillion* in particular is concerned, there has not been a full
reconciliation between that and *The Lord of the Rings*: not
only are the tone and area of concern different (quite properly so), but on such things as the origin of the Orcs, one
book must be wrong (presumably *The Lord of the Rings*) and
one right. Either the Enemy bred the Orcs in mockery of the
Elves (*The Lord of the Rings*) or he captured and perverted
Elves (*The Silmarillion*), and even if we accept the capture
theory, explaining away the statement in the earlier book, we
are left with the fact that the Orcs in *The Lord of the Rings*
do not sound like Elves in any way, shape, or form. Mockery
perhaps, but perverted from Elves, I think not.

In any event, we are considering not Tolkien's appeal,
or his achievement, in general, but in this one specific work,
different in kind from all his others. I would like to give here
some idea of the effect that work has had on me, serving as
specimen where I may fail as a literary critic. Let me do so
by telling you a story.

In 1967-8 there was a used-book store on State Street
in Madison, Wisconsin, not far from the library. While I was
browsing, I noticed a dog-eared card, posted on the bulletin
board, advertising the University of Wisconsin Tolkien Society, and giving the name of its president, Mr. Richard West.
I called him (he had, characteristically, forgotten the very
existence of the card on the bulletin board) and shortly
thereafter went to a meeting of the society. In that society
there was a community of spirit as well as of interest. From
The Lord of the Rings grew friendship.

The word "grew" is important, of course, but more important was, and is, the friendship. C. S. Lewis, better than
most, has described the growth and particular characteristics of friendship, using Tolkien as one of his examples. The
critical characteristic is the shared interest, the critical moment its discovery. And if my own experience is represen-
tative, part of the appeal of *The Lord of the Rings* is not only
that those who read and revel in it become friends from the
moment of meeting, but that they feel themselves Tolkien's

friends. This, doubtless, was hard on him: it cannot be easy to have millions of friends one has never met, especially when they call on one without warning or call one long distance in the middle of the night. Tolkien eventually went into seclusion to avoid the importunities of his admirers— which is itself testimony to the degree to which *The Lord of the Rings* caught them in its web.

The world has changed since those days. Tolkien no longer lives in Oxford, or indeed in the circles of this world. Conferences on Middle Earth no longer meet on midwestern campuses. The long-awaited *Silmarillion*, though Professor Tolkien himself failed to finish it, is awaited no more. There is no longer a Tolkien Society of America, it having been taken into the Mythopoeic Society in California. *The Lord of the Rings* is no longer a discovery, or even a cult book. It has, more or less, been brought to the movie screen: that which we so greatly feared has come upon us.

But somewhere (and I do not apologize for borrowing these words) there is a corner of our mind where it is always 1966, with the Tolkiens at 76 Sandfield Road, and always the Great Years in the Third Age of Middle Earth. The timeless moment forever intersects our lives—both lives, in both times. "When Anodos looked through the door of the timeless, he brought back no message." But when John Ronald Reuel Tolkien looked through that door, he brought us back *The Lord of the Rings*.

> In endless English comfort, by country-folk caressed,
> I left the old three-decker at the Islands of the Blest.
>   Rudyard Kipling, "The Three-Decker"

BIBLIOGRAPHICAL NOTE

FOR two reasons, it does not seem particularly worthwhile for me to append a detailed bibliography to this commentary. First, my approach is based very largely on *The Lord of the Rings* itself, and secondarily on clues from C. S. Lewis or from Tolkien's other work—almost all of which is quite well known. Second, there is a magnificent annotated checklist of Tolkien criticism (revised edition) now out from Kent State University Press, and it would be superfluous of me to do in brief what Mr. Richard West has therein done in such detail.

Nevertheless, I should (1) provide a few references and (2) note those critics whose approach has something in common with mine. Readers will find Mr. Colin Wilson's remarks (referred to in Chapter I) in his *Tree by Tolkien*, and Mr. Brian Aldiss's in his entertaining *Billion Year Spree*. Both are available in paperback. Lewis's view of Haggard is found in his *Time & Tide* notice on Morton Cohen's biography: Tolkien's is found (as noted) in an interview with Henry Resnick, printed in the fanzine *Niekas* in 1967. And readers searching for critics whose approaches resemble mine are referred (among the living) to the aforementioned Mr. West and Mrs. Deborah Rogers.

Both of these have essays in *A Tolkien Compass*, Mr. West's (on polyphonic narrative) being in my view the single finest piece of literary criticism devoted to *The Lord of the Rings* by a living critic; Mrs. Rogers' contribution I have mentioned in the text (in Chapter III). She is also the author of the Twayne's English Authors Series book on Tolkien (1980).

Both Mr. West and Mrs. Rogers were, with me, members of the University of Wisconsin Tolkien Society in the 1960s.

Mr. Carpenter's biography is, of course, invaluable; there are some worthwhile essays in some of the collections; Clyde Kilby's work is attractive, as, generally, is Charles Huttar's (both of these men, it will be noted, are active in the Conference on Christianity and Literature); also worthwhile is Professor Kocher's work on *The Lord of the Rings.*